JANELLE ESTES | ANDY MACMILLAN

# USER
# TESTED

HOW THE WORLD'S
TOP COMPANIES USE
**HUMAN INSIGHT** TO
**CREATE GREAT EXPERIENCES**

WILEY

Published by John Wiley & Sons, Inc., Hoboken, New Jersey.
Published simultaneously in Canada.

For general information on our other products and services or for technical support, please contact our Customer Care Department within the United States at (800) 762-2974, outside the United States at (317) 572-3993 or fax (317) 572-4002.

Wiley publishes in a variety of print and electronic formats and by print-on-demand. Some material included with standard print versions of this book may not be included in e-books or in print-on-demand. If this book refers to media such as a CD or DVD that is not included in the version you purchased, you may download this material at http://booksupport.wiley.com. For more information about Wiley products, visit www.wiley.com.

*Library of Congress Cataloging-in-Publication Data*

Names: Estes, Janelle, author. | MacMillan, Andy (Andy P.), author.
Title: User tested : how the world's top companies use human insight to
   create great experiences / Janelle Estes and Andy MacMillan.
Description: Hoboken, New Jersey : Wiley, [2022] | Includes index.
Identifiers: LCCN 2021045160 (print) | LCCN 2021045161 (ebook) | ISBN
   9781119844631 (hardback) | ISBN 9781119844730 (adobe pdf) | ISBN
   9781119844723 (epub)
Subjects: LCSH: Customer relations.
Classification: LCC HF5415.5 .E77 2022  (print) | LCC HF5415.5 (ebook) |
   DDC 658.8/12—dc23
LC record available at https://lccn.loc.gov/2021045160
LC ebook record available at https://lccn.loc.gov/2021045161

Cover Design: Wiley
Cover Images: © Rubber Stamp Text: © Tetiana Lazunova/Getty Images, Check Mark:
          © Giorgio Morara/Shutterstock

SKY10031385_122821

*This book is dedicated to the visionary individuals and organizations that have been studying and championing the importance of human insight for decades across the fields of cognitive science, human factors, ergonomics, and human-computer interaction. Their work on merging and maturing the practices of user-centered design, human factors, and user experience has paved the way for our work, including what we've written here.*

*These trail blazers all embraced the belief that things should be designed to suit humans, instead of forcing humans to adapt to poor design. This belief was important in the early days of aviation; influential during the age of manufacturing and physical experiences; and is became absolutely critical in the current economy of personal computers and digital interaction.*

*Darrell Benatar and Dave Garr, UserTesting's visionary founders, belong on the list of thought-leaders, and this book couldn't have been written without their commitment to genuine customer-centricity. These two recognized the need for fast, reliable human insight way back in 1999, and have been advocating for its inclusion in all business decisions ever since. By helping companies experience what their customers experience, Dave and Darrell have changed the face of business. For the better. And we owe them a huge debt of gratitude.*

# Contents

LIST OF FIGURES    **xi**

ACKNOWLEDGMENTS    **xiii**

PREFACE    **xv**

**Part 1    The Challenge:** Understanding Customers as Humans, Not Data Points    **1**

1  **Competing in the Experience Economy:** Many Companies Succeed Despite Sub-Par Customer Understanding    **3**
2  **The Missing Dimension:** Why and How Human Insight Powers Great Experiences    **21**

**Part 2    The Solution:** Human Insight Powers Customer-Centric Actions    **41**

3  **What're You Trying to Answer?** Mapping a User Test Approach to Your Desired Learnings    **43**
4  **You Are Not Your Customer:** How to Get Access to the Perspectives That Matter    **63**
5  **Capture and Analyze:** Sifting Through the Noise to Find the Signal    **75**
6  **Take Action on Human Insight:** Decide Where and How to Apply Your Learnings    **89**

**Part 3    The Playbook:** How Human Insight Fits into Your Business    **97**

7  **Product Development:** Creating Products People Love    **99**
8  **Marketing:** Getting Inside the Heads of Your Buyers    **121**
9  **Every Team Owns the Experience:** Optimizing the Holistic Customer Journey    **149**

# Part 4 The Culture Shift: Applying Human Insight at Scale 173

**10 Bottom Up:** The Grassroots Movement **175**

**11 Top Down:** How Executives Can Support and Model Change **191**

ONE FINAL NOTE **205**

INDEX **207**

# List of Figures

**Figure 1.1**   Customer Understanding Trends Over Time   **9**

**Figure 2.1**   Effectiveness Shown with Big Data and Human Insight   **29**

**Figure 2.2**   Ease Shown with Big Data and Human Insight   **31**

**Figure 2.3**   Emotion Shown with Big Data and Human Insight   **33**

**Figure 2.4**   Human Insight Provides Multiple Human Signals   **35**

**Figure 3.1**   Mapping Your Question to a Topline Business Driver   **46**

**Figure 3.2**   The Design Thinking Framework   **50**

**Figure 3.3**   Too Many Broad Questions in a User Test Can Overwhelm   **57**

**Figure 5.1**   2×2 Matrix to Prioritize Issues Uncovered in User Tests   **87**

**Figure 7.1**   Jen Cardello's Product Development Framework   **101**

**Figure 8.1**   Using Human Insight to Inform Your Marketing Efforts   **122**

**Figure 8.2**   Empathy Map   **128**

**Figure 9.1**   Using Human Insight Across the Holistic Customer Journey   **150**

# Acknowledgments

We would like to thank all of the individuals and organizations that helped make this book possible.

First, thank you to our customers who let us share their stories and bring the power of human insight to life.

Thanks to everyone at UserTesting for the work you do every day.

Thanks to Richard Narramore and Deborah Schindlar at Wiley.

Thanks to Ethan Beute at BombBomb, Laura Baverman at Pendo, and Dan Steinman, Robin Merritt, and Nick Mehta at Gainsight for your guidance.

Huge thanks to Sally McGraw for your expertise, guidance, and support throughout.

And finally, thanks to our families, who gave us the encouragement, space, and time we needed to dedicate to this work. We love you.

# Preface

Imagine...

*... You sit down to your annual company meeting and before the CEO even speaks, you're captivated by a video of your very own customers talking about how much they love the experiences you provide. And suggestions on how to make the experience better ...*

*... Your company launches a new product and everyone at your company has access to customer feedback through a shared Slack channel. In the channel, you can watch real customers using the new product and sharing their perspectives ...*

*... Anytime you'd like, you're given the opportunity to connect with customers yourself. You can ask for their opinions and get input on any aspect of your work quickly and easily ...*

*... Your organization has an internal app that streams curated videos of customers using the experiences you provide. Employees can subscribe to channels: the most-watched customer videos, feedback from specific customer segments such as "top spenders," and a competitive intelligence channel ...*

*... Your customers can opt in or volunteer to provide these rich perspectives, and freely do so because they're invested in the experience you provide and want to make it better ...*

*... Once a month, you're asked to weigh in on what customer segments should be tested or which questions should be asked when customer perspectives are gathered. For example, you get to upvote competitive testing or downvote testing of a new ad campaign depending on what will help you most ...*

*... You get to the office in the morning, grab a cup of coffee in the kitchen, and you are immediately enthralled by a video of a customer on a flatscreen above the coffee maker. You get to watch a real customer as they view and react to a recently launched marketing campaign ...*

*...Every Friday, you get an alert on your phone reminding you to watch this week's most commented-on video of a customer using one of your competitor's experiences ...*

And imagine this is all done in an effort to create a company-wide, shared understanding of who your customers are as human beings, not data points, so you can make better, more empathetic decisions. So you can bring humanity into the business. And so you can do it in a way that enables everyone to build a true and meaningful connection to the customers they serve.

This shared understanding ultimately helps people at your company act with more urgency and with the needs of the customer infusing every discussion, activity, and decision. And not only is there a shared understanding, but there's also a shared *desire* to augment that understanding so the business can continually learn about and improve upon the experiences it provides.

But this is not how businesses have traditionally operated. For far too long, we have relied on understanding our customers—who they are, what they do, what they need—in the form of big data, analytics, and surveys. And while this information is valuable, it's incomplete. We're missing a critical dimension. We're missing the human perspective.

What is it actually like to *be* my customer? What is it like to see the world through their eyes? Walmart founder Sam Walton is famous for "walking the aisles" at his stores to get an on-the-ground look at his customers and how his business operated, but most teams don't have access to this perspective today. That will change. It has to.

We're living in an age where customers are in control, yet we're simultaneously losing touch with them. As the world continues to digitally transform at lightspeed and tech continues to physically separate us from our customers, the divide between our teams and the customers we serve will continue to grow.

So what do we do? How do we fill this gap? The answer is simple. We need to bring authentic customer perspectives back into key decisions. We need to pair the myriads of data we have at our fingertips with the *literal* voice of the customer. We need to connect with our customers, human to human, so we can make decisions that deliver better experiences.

*We need human insight.*

# Meet the Authors

## Janelle Estes, Chief Insights Officer

I've been fascinated by human behavior my entire life. My mom has said when I was about three years old, she'd take me to the grocery store, wheel me around in the front of the cart and watch me observe everyone around me with a keen eye. Then, a week or more later, I'd say, "Mom ... that guy at the store in the red shirt? Why was he buying four boxes of Cheerios?" She marveled both at my ability to retain detail and my questioning mind: Why was I thinking about these things? Why did I care?

It's because people are amazing and quirky and utterly intriguing, and I've always wanted to better understand them. So I studied the fascinating intersection between cognitive science, human factors, and design. I worked at Nielsen Norman Group and Forrester as a researcher and UX specialist, often running lab-based user testing that took weeks to complete. (Translation: I was deeply nerdy about this stuff long before it had any cachet.) I decided to move to User-Testing when I saw more and more companies adopt remote user testing solutions, and I've seen a massive shift in how companies connect with their customers—through tech-enabled solutions—to meet the speed and scale required for business today.

Regardless of how this work is done, I have seen the "lightbulb" go off time and time again when people observe user tests, and it never fails to inspire me. As someone who has always believed in the importance of human insight, it's been amazing to watch my field of expertise grow from a little niche superpower to something that many companies see as hugely valuable and business-critical.

Yet there is still so much untapped potential; we can grow exponentially from here. My passion for bringing humanity back into business decisions hasn't waned, and I see this book as the perfect way to engage an even wider audience.

## Andy MacMillan, CEO

The importance of customer feedback especially resonates with me because I've spent my entire career in software product development. As a former product executive at Oracle and Salesforce, I saw first-hand the critical role that customer understanding plays in creating great experiences. Technology does amazing things but it's where technology meets people—the customer experience—that makes technology most valuable to us as individuals. And I've learned that the secret to doing this is putting the customer and their interests at the center of every decision.

As the CEO of UserTesting, I genuinely love giving companies the ability to find and interact with their own customers in a way that facilitates human insight on any aspect of the experience they provide. And I know that ability is a critical one in the modern marketplace, as the speed of technology has often eclipsed the quality of the human interactions with that technology. Putting your customers at the center of your experiences can change that.

# What to Expect from This Book

We've structured this book to be as approachable and pragmatic as possible.

Part 1 offers some background on how businesses became obsessed with numbers, stopped talking to customers, and why this trend can't persist. It is illustrated with plenty of great case studies and examples.

Part 2 is about the basics of capturing human insight through the practice of user testing, including how to find the right people, how to ask the right questions, how to make sense of what you capture, how to build a shared understanding, and how to take action based on your learnings.

Part 3 is a detailed playbook that walks you through a wide variety of ways to collect human insight and how they can be pulled into various parts of your business, including marketing efforts, product development, and beyond.

Part 4 is about spurring that all-important culture change within your organization to incorporate human insight everywhere, all the time.

Our hope is that, in reading this book, you'll help us build a better, brighter, customer-focused future. It'll be one where companies pull human insight into their everyday work and decision-making, organically and consistently.

That's the future we envision, and it's well within reach right now. All we have to do is commit to deepening our understanding of our customers by truly observing and listening to what they're telling us and using that to make well-informed, customer-centric decisions.

It's difficult to predict the technologies and experiences that will emerge in the coming years, but one thing is certain: Human insight is the key to staying connected to our customers in the Experience Economy.[1]

---

[1]This term is gradually entering common use, but was first coined by Joseph Pine II and James H. Gilmore in a 1998 *Harvard Business Review* article titled, "Welcome to the Experience Economy." It's fascinating, and well worth a read ... though we'll explore many of its high points in chapters to come.

# PART 1

# The Challenge: Understanding Customers as Humans, Not Data Points

# CHAPTER 1

# Competing in the Experience Economy

## Many Companies Succeed Despite Sub-Par Customer Understanding

Are customers at the heart of your business?

No business leader in their right mind would answer, "No," but the sad truth is that many of us in the corporate world have been paying lip service to customer needs, ideas, and feedback without deeply understanding and taking action on them.

This inertia is, in part, created by the speed of innovation. As the digital world has emerged and evolved, it's enabled businesses to reach size and scale faster than ever before, and to do so with smaller initial investments and fewer people.

Instead of sinking tens of thousands of dollars into a neighborhood gym full of costly equipment and overhead, we can spend a couple hundred bucks on designing a fitness app that helps people slim down and build muscle mass.

Instead of attempting to build an entirely new academic institution, we can compile expertise and information into an online learning platform.

Instead of spending two years scouting locations, finding suppliers, and negotiating contracts to launch a brick-and-mortar retail business, we can spend two days tweaking our ecommerce infrastructure and supply chain.

The acceleration rate is dizzying. You know this already.

You also know that the ability to go from zero to profit in record time has triggered a tsunami of businesses, many of which offer nearly identical products. In this teeming marketplace, the key differentiator and driver of loyalty has become the customer *experience*.

Does the customer feel understood and valued? Can they set up a new account without any friction? Is the initial experience using the app easy and enjoyable? Are the new offers that appear in their inboxes anticipating their needs and helping them feel connected to the company?

Today's customers expect great experiences with the products, services, and brands that they support. Many of the businesses that have achieved phenomenal success in this market are the ones that know this and prioritize the creation of above-and-beyond customer experiences.

Take Spotify: Personalization has always been central to the music streaming service's brand and market presence, and in the summer of 2021, Spotify kicked it up a notch by launching its "Only You" campaign. This dedicated in-app experience leverages user listening data to highlight the artists, songs, genres, and listening patterns that are unique and important to each listener.

Like the service's popular and personalized year-end summary, Spotify Wrapped, Only You content is easily shareable across social media. The Only You content joins Discover Weekly, Release Radar, and Daily Mixes in the app's Made for You hub, the title of which underlines Spotify's dedication to making each user's experience feel personal, bespoke, and special.[1]

Spotify has become one of the most successful on-demand music platforms globally, with more than 320 million active daily users and more than 144 million paying monthly subscribers as of 2021,[2] while competitor Pandora has shrunk to 55.9 million active monthly users and 6.4 million subscribers.[3] This focus on the almighty listener has clearly contributed to its success, and more and more people prefer and expect to receive personalization at this level.

And their expectations continue to rise as they compare experiences, not just within the same category, but across all of the products, services, and brands that they consume and support.

For example, when consumers purchase clothing online, they may compare their ordering and store pick-up experience with the experience they have booking a restaurant reservation via a smartphone app. The intuitive and fast reservation experience doesn't resemble the retail transaction, but the consumer doesn't care. They've come to expect the same level of ease and integration from both.

Nailing this mix of canny design and well-timed emotional ephemera can set a company apart from its competitors. *Far* apart. Think trillions of miles.

---

[1]https://www.thedrum.com/opinion/2021/06/29/hit-them-the-feels-how-generate-emotive-customer-experiences
[2]https://www.digitaltrends.com/music/spotify-vs-pandora/
[3]https://musically.com/2021/04/29/pandora-ended-q1-2021-with-55-9m-monthly-active-listeners/

It's all borne out in the stats. Research shows that customers consistently convert for companies who offer them delightful experiences, and that they remain loyal to those companies once a connection is made. Even if another company offers similar products or services at lower cost or delivers them faster, people prefer the company that delivers the best experience and makes an authentic connection.

Take air travel as an example: Overall, airlines consistently rank as one of the top five most hated industries in the United States,[4] so the bar is set pretty low. The advent of fees for things like checked bags and more legroom has continued to sour public opinion, in part because when customers have to pay for something that used to be free, they interpret this as a personal loss.[5]

And yet the U.S. Travel Association found that 60 percent of travelers would welcome additional fees dedicated to improving efficiency and choice.[6] During the COVID-19 outbreak, surveyed travelers said they would pay up to 17 percent more to fly on airlines that blocked the middle seat,[7] and when Delta continued the blocked-seat policy after other airlines rescinded it, Delta rose to number one in the American Customer Satisfaction Index.[8]

This is a single example, but it isn't unique. Brands with superior customer experience rake in 5.7 times more revenue than competitors

---

[4]https://www.forbes.com/sites/blakemorgan/2018/10/16/top-5-most-hated-industries-by-customers/?sh=72ec6eec90b5
[5]https://hbr.org/2021/06/how-airlines-can-cut-costs-without-annoying-customers
[6]https://www.ustravel.org/press/survey-travelers-willing-pay-more-improve-flying-experience
[7]https://www.businessinsider.com/airlines-middle-seat-social-distance-coronavirus-delta-2020-8
[8]https://www.theacsi.org/index.php?option=com_content&view=article&id=147&catid=&Itemid=212&i=Airlines

who lag behind,[9] and 73 percent of customers say that good experiences influence their brand loyalties.[10] And since every MBA knows it's far more costly to acquire new customers than it is to keep loyal ones happy, this is news worth noting.

Yet far too many business leaders note it and are paralyzed by the prospect of trying to please these hordes of tech-savvy, highly discerning consumers. Either that, or they pour company money into analytics, surveys, and customer databases and assume an influx of data will help them rise as a market leader.

It won't. Not by a long shot.

Many companies spend billions of dollars collecting, sorting, and interpreting customer data, but still don't fully understand the people those data represent.

They may formulate potential new products or features to solve a customer problem, but do so without understanding *how* the problem arose or *why* it's a problem worth solving.

They may segment the living daylights out of their customer lists but still struggle to understand drivers and motivating factors.

They may sit inside dashboards watching app downloads and conversion rates, but they don't know why people are opting to download a competitor's app instead of theirs or dropping out of the purchase funnel.

---

[9]https://www.retailcustomerexperience.com/blogs/why-personalization-is-key-for-retail-customer-experiences/
[10]https://www.pwc.com/future-of-cx

*A whopping eighty-four percent of customers say their interactions with organizations fall short of their expectations,*[11] *proof that we're missing a crucial piece of the puzzle.*

The missing puzzle piece is a view into authentic customer perspectives: the ability to stand in the shoes of a customer, to see through their eyes, hear what they have to say, and understand what it feels like for them to interact with a company.

The missing puzzle piece is human insight.

## When Did We Start to Value Data Over Human Connections?

Before we dig into the mindset shifts and strategies that will help you transform your business through capturing human insight, we need to understand how we got here.

What caused so many businesses to *stop* talking with and observing their customers? When did we lose sight of the importance of seeing the world through our customers' eyes? Or did we ever really have these things in the first place?

Here's a quick summary of how companies have shifted their customer understanding efforts over the last century or so, mainly in response to new tech and manufacturing advancements.

----

[11]https://www.gartner.com/en/newsroom/press-releases/2018-10-03-gartner-survey-finds-that-most-consumers-have-underwhelming-digital-experiences

| Dates | Era | Business Drivers | Customer Understanding Efforts |
|---|---|---|---|
| 1900–1690 | Age of Manufacturing | Quality products Efficiency of build | In this era, the customer is considered a repository for consumables. Organizations are performing some informal word-of-mouth polling, but don't have a formal approach to customer understanding |
| 1960–1990 | Age of Distribution | Supply chain Ability to sell globally Reaching more buyers | As the seeds of the global economy are planted during this period, corporations are becoming more invested in buyer and customer input since they are attempting to sell to new and unfamiliar populations. Marketing research and an early Voice of Customer methodology emerge and rise in popularity. |
| 1990–2010 | Age of Information | E-commerce speed | Tracking clicks and purchases, then correlating behaviors with preferences gradually overtakes more traditional (and personal) methods of customer understanding. Digital experiences disintermediate customers from the teams building and supporting them. |
| 2010–Present | Age of the Customer | Differentiation Brand experience Buying expeience | As the world shifts to primarily digital experiences, the customer is in the driver's seat. Companies are forced to change how they interact with customers, support and anticipate their needs, and deliver exceptional experiences. |

**FIGURE 1.1**   Customer Understanding Trends Over Time

*Source for dates and era names: Forrester Research, Inc., Competitive Strategy in the Age of the Customer, October 2013*[12]

So we've arrived in the Age of the Customer in the Experience Economy, an era in which consumers desire experiences and businesses respond by explicitly designing and promoting them.[13]

[12]https://www.forrester.com/report/competitive-strategy-in-the-age-of-the-customer/RES59159

[13]https://hbr.org/1998/07/welcome-to-the-experience-economy

Business consultants B. Joseph Pine II and James H. Gilmore first defined the Experience Economy in *Harvard Business Review* back in 1998, and their definition has become increasingly relevant as the world has become more and more digitized.

Modern customers interact with the Experience Economy by making decisions that fit their lifestyles and values and paying for products and services that not only meet but exceed their expectations. If a certain company isn't up to snuff, they can easily find another that is.[14]

This fickleness came to a head during the COVID-19 outbreak of 2020. In a study conducted by McKinsey & Company, 40 percent of respondents said they'd changed brands as a result of the pandemic, double the level of brand switching from 2019. Convenience was cited as a main driver of shopping behavior change—which makes sense during a time period when normal consumer activity was restricted—but 40 percent of respondents also said they were seeking brands that matched with their values.[15] Clearly, people are more than willing to abandon a once-beloved brand if it fails to deliver the level of experience or values they want and expect.

Keeping up with this shifting set of customer demands is overwhelming and costly, so many enterprises have chosen to leverage their gargantuan stockpiles of carefully collected customer data: repeat purchases, loyalty program sign-ups, requests or preferences that have been codified through apps, websites, or customer service interactions. Doing this feels easier, faster, and cheaper than connecting with customers in person, and many business leaders have been led to believe that it's more accurate to rely on hard numbers than subjective input like customer stories and direct observations.

---

[14]Drawn from: https://www.usertesting.com/blog/age-of-the-customer?
[15]https://www.mckinsey.com/business-functions/marketing-and-sales/our-insights/survey-us-consumer-sentiment-during-the-coronavirus-crisis

Surveys have replaced casual conversations with customers, databases have replaced shop-a-longs, and analytics have replaced observing your customers in real time. Instead of making decisions based on a blend of both numbers and customer narratives, many companies have opted to just trust the numbers.

This is how we find ourselves living in an era when customers are more influential and empowered than ever before and largely ignored by the companies that serve them. According to *Harvard Business Review*, product managers spend about 7 percent of their time interacting with customers.[16] CEOs give an average of 3 percent of their schedules to the buying public.[17] This is how we end up with enterprises insisting they're "customer-centric" when they haven't reached out to an actual customer in months. Sometimes years.

No wonder the select few companies who actually *do* solicit and incorporate customer input have rocketed ahead of their data-myopic competitors.

## Great Experiences Are Derived from Deep Customer Understanding

Historically, buying a used car has been an objectively miserable experience. It's a long, drawn-out process that often involves traipsing across huge lots at multiple dealerships, test-driving dozens of vehicles, finally settling on one that's the right model but the wrong color, wondering how much of the crucial car back-story you're actually getting, then finally signing reams of indecipherable

---

[16]https://productmanagementfestival.com/wp-content/uploads/2019/08/Trends-Benchmarks-in-Product-Management-2019.pdf
[17]https://hbr.org/2018/07/the-leaders-calendar

paperwork. It's so bad, studies have shown that 81 percent of consumers do not enjoy the car-buying process.[18]

And, of course, there are the salespeople whose profession has spawned an entire genre of derisive humor. A Gallup poll found that a measly 1 percent judge car salespeople as highly trustworthy.[19]

Paints a pretty dismal picture, doesn't it?

And yet used cars are big business. Nearly 41 million used vehicles sold in the United States in the year 2019, with average transaction price hitting an all-time record high of $20,618.[20] The market size, measured by revenue, was $153.1 billion in early 2021.[21] If someone unearthed the buyer pain points and addressed them, they could make bank. And that's just what the founders of Carvana did.

In 2012, this Phoenix-based tech startup decided to change the game, not because the founders had a problem they wanted to address but because they recognized a problem that millions of car-buyers across the world all shared. Carvana wanted to make the used car-buying process simpler and more enjoyable.

"When we built Carvana, it wasn't just, 'Let's go find something that's not online and bring it there.' We realized that the customer experience of buying a car ... people don't love it. It takes a lot of time," says Ryan Keeton, co-founder and chief brand officer at the company.[22]

---

[18]http://info.dealersocket.com/rs/827-YDT-828/images/iDAR%202016%20Pages%20-%20Web.pdf
[19]https://news.gallup.com/poll/1654/honesty-ethics-professions.aspx
[20]https://static.ed.edmunds-media.com/unversioned/img/industry-center/insights/2019-used-vehicle-report.pdf
[21]https://www.ibisworld.com/industry-statistics/market-size/used-car-dealers-united-states/
[22]https://www.insidehook.com/article/vehicles/carvana-interview-buying-cars-online

Yes, Keeton and his co-founders set out to create a business model with reduced overall costs that would pass savings on to the consumer through lower prices with no hidden fees, but they also wanted to delight used car buyers. They wanted to build a fun, easy way to shop, finance, and trade in cars that took the slog out of the process.

So they created a website and app that provide 360-degree views of the interior and exterior of each car so customers can inspect potential vehicles without ever stepping onto a used car lot. The company buys and inspects every vehicle they list, enabling them to offer an unprecedented seven-day return policy on all cars. Carvana offers auto loans directly, giving users access to personalized financing terms without hurting their credit scores. Customers can browse through tens of thousands of listings and schedule next-day delivery or pickup.

And if they choose pickup, it'll be at a vending machine. No, really.

In 2014, Carvana introduced its first multi-story car vending machine in Atlanta and expanded to twenty-seven by 2021. The structures provide an unforgettable signature experience for customers who have completed the online purchasing process and opted to pick up their vehicle on-site. All they have to do is show up, claim their one-pound golden token, and drop it into the slot to release their car. The company came up with this idea early on and partnered with design firms in Germany and the United States to make it a reality.[23] The vending machines have become branding icons for Carvana, and the quirky experience they offer reinforces the company's desire to make car-buying fun.

The one-two punch of convenience and enjoyability has paid off, and customers continually rave about their positive experiences working with Carvana. When we spoke to some of them, they were overwhelmingly enthusiastic.

---

[23]https://www.salesforce.com/products/service-cloud/resources/carvana/

*"It was so simple. It was easy to find the vehicle I wanted. Getting it delivered was nice. Honestly, everything about the car buying experience was good."*

*—Carvana customer*

*"I never had to leave my house. I didn't have to be haggled by salespeople. They just delivered it when it was convenient for me. It was really easy."*

*—Carvana customer*

"You have to start with the economics. What does the customer want and need? Is there a way to provide that more efficiently than the rest of the market does? For us, the answer was yes," explains Ernie Garcia III, Carvana's president, CEO, and chairman. "Once you have better economics, you can also build a culture of delivering great experiences to your customers on top of that, and that is exactly what we seek to do every day."[24]

Carvana has become the second largest used car retailer in the United States over its short history, and the future looks bright. The company's stock prices have risen consistently and sales jumped 43 percent in 2020, despite (or perhaps because of) the global pandemic.[25] If Carvana can continue to create and deliver delightful and unique experiences to used-car buyers, it's got a shot at sustainable success.

# But … You Can't Always Take Customer Suggestions at Face Value

Another customer experience champion, Target, has been studying shopper preferences for decades and adapting to shifting needs. The big box retailer has become legendary for coaxing more money

---

[24]https://www.entrepreneur.com/article/328646
[25]https://www.autonews.com/used-cars/carvana-q4-net-loss-widens-debt-costs-revenue-surges

out of in-store shoppers' wallets than they'd planned to spend. We spoke with a few Target regulars who described this serendipitous shopping experience with cheerful resignation:

> *"I pass the accessories and see something I need. Then I go to the clothing section, and then I have to walk through the home goods. There is a feeling I shouldn't be doing this because I am going to see something I'm going to want to buy. It is the excitement of finding something. . ."*
>
> —*Target customer*

> *"They have so much no matter what you need. You go in looking for chips and you spend $500."*
>
> —*Target customer*

In recent years, Target has invested heavily in creating a seamless omnichannel experience, ensuring its customers get the same level of service regardless of how they interact with the brand. Starting in 2017, the corporation strategically invested $7 billion to overhaul its supply chain, invest in digital transformation, and reinvent the in-store experience.

Knowing that the in-person shopper was an important part of their business strategy, CEO Brian Cornell said, "We're putting our stores at the center of our strategy. We spent more than $4 billion remodeling our stores, completing hundreds each year, transforming them into showrooms, fulfillment hubs, and service centers."

Enhancements included in-person pick-up and drive-up for orders placed online, and same-day delivery via Shipt (which Target acquired in 2017). These options boosted the retailer's digital sales growth, which jumped 24 percent to $8.34 billion in 2020.[26] Not too shabby.

---

[26]https://blog.lengow.com/target-omnichannel-retail-success/

In an interesting twist, Cornell declared that this transformation strategy was based on customer feedback and opinions, which were mostly that brick-and-mortar stores are *so* last century.

"We had every reason to believe this would work, because we've been doing our homework; testing these bets and listening to our guests," Cornell said. "And for them, stores were dead. They were just boring and uninspiring. Our guests still loved our brand. They just wanted us to do more."[27]

Translation: Target leadership hypothesized that abandoning their stores altogether would fail, and decided to upgrade and enhance the physical locations while also creating multiple ways for customers to buy from the brand, quickly and easily. Since Target has become the poster child for omnichannel strategy, they clearly made the right call.

This shows that listening to and analyzing what your customers have expressed is a crucial first step, but the final piece of the puzzle is interpreting feedback and identifying the issues it surfaces.

It requires teasing out the real human insight, which may seem hidden at first.

Customers told Target that stores were boring, but Target didn't just shutter its physical locations; instead, internal teams drilled down into the customer insights and addressed the real problem. If stores are boring, don't abandon them. Make them better, more fun, more accessible, and easier to incorporate into your life.

---

[27]https://diginomica.com/digital-growth-slows-target-stays-target-ongoing-omni-channel-transformation

# Decisioning on Metrics Alone Puts You at Risk

Truly customer-centric decision making is derived from understanding what it is like to actually *be* your customer. It's informed by information about what the customer sees, values, and observes as they interact with you. It's depth of detail paired with emotional authenticity.

Without human insight, you put your company in very real danger of charging off in the wrong direction, and you may:

- **Build products no one wants:** Bic released the Bic For Her line of pens marketed directly to women in 2012. The pens were met with a wave of ridicule from customers and media outlets alike.[28]

- **Make uninformed decisions about current offerings, changing them in ways that frustrate or alienate users:** In 2018, social media app Snapchat split the app interface into two sections, consolidating friend content on the left side, media content on the right, and installing a handful of other design changes. Users were so furious, the app lost 3 million daily users over the following three months.[29]

- **Become increasingly detached from the people you serve:** When exercise bike company Peloton learned that many husbands buy their products as gifts for their wives, they created a commercial in which a woman gets a Peloton from her spouse as a holiday gift. The ad sparked viral backlash from people

---

[28]https://www.forbes.com/sites/davidvinjamuri/2012/08/30/bic-for-her-what-they-were-actually-thinking-as-told-by-a-man-who-worked-on-tampons/?sh=23fd75193ab8
[29]https://www.altpress.com/news/snapchat-losing-users-tech/

who felt it had both sexist and body-shaming themes, and the company's stock fell by 9 percent in response.[30]

- **Erode employee satisfaction:** Multiple studies have shown that happy customers make for happy employees, and miserable customers can cause mass employee exodus.[31]

- **Miss out on key opportunities:** The classic example here is Kodak. The company pioneered many of the underlying technologies inherent to digital cameras, creating some core components as early as 1975. But they didn't ask their customers to weigh in, assumed digital was a fad, and doubled down on film. Now the company is all but obsolete.[32]

# Integrating Human Insight into Decisioning Is the Way Forward

When you act on customer understanding powered by human insight paired with data, you gain:

- **More market share:** After the company hit rock bottom in 2008, Domino's Pizza took customer feedback to heart: they completely changed their recipes (which people hated), and invested in creating a fun and easy digital ordering experience. Between 2010 and 2017, Domino's stock has appreciated more than 2,000 percent, outperforming Alphabet, Amazon, Apple, and Netflix.[33]

- **Customer loyalty and die-hard fans:** Online retailer Zappos has always lauded themselves as a customer-first organization

---

[30]https://www.nytimes.com/2019/12/03/business/peloton-bike-ad-stock.html
[31]https://hbr.org/2019/08/the-key-to-happy-customers-happy-employees
[32]https://www.businessinsider.com/this-man-invented-the-digital-camera-in-1975-and-his-bosses-at-kodak-never-let-it-see-the-light-of-day-2015-8
[33]https://www.fool.com/investing/2017/04/04/how-digital-innovation-delivered-2000-gains-for-do.aspx

and their dedication to soliciting and acting upon feedback has won them the loyalty of millions. Nearly 75 percent of Zappos purchases come from returning customers.[34]

- **Increased efficiency and lower costs:** Analyzing almost two decades of data from 128 firms, researchers found that higher customer satisfaction can lower future cost of sales.[35]

- **A company culture that attracts and retains talent:** Southwest Airlines has long been known as an organization that values customer input and satisfaction, as well as one that bends over backwards to keep its workforce happy. The company has a 96 percent retention rate and has never laid off a single employee.[36] The result is everyone wants to work for them. Southwest receives a new job application every two seconds.[37]

- **Expanded worldview and inclusivity:** When a company in the feminine care space launched a new product, internal research teams spoke with "traditional" customers but also interviewed trans men and trans women about their needs and preferences. This yielded insights that the client company would have otherwise missed.[38]

As these examples illustrate, data alone will not help you build unforgettable customer experiences, secure undying loyalty, or improve your offerings in meaningful ways. Data may help you see the big picture—generally in the form of trends and patterns—but human insight adds color and context, giving a human perspective that you can't get from the numbers.

---

[34]https://www.forbes.com/sites/languatica/2012/05/31/delivering-happiness-why-at-zappos-its-your-birthday-every-day/?sh=72429bc85f00
[35]https://www.ama.org/2020/06/11/customer-satisfaction-and-its-impact-on-the-future-costs-of-selling/
[36]https://www.humansynergistics.com/blog/culture-university/details/culture-university/2018/05/29/southwest-airlines-reveals-5-culture-lessons
[37]https://hbr.org/2015/12/how-southwest-airlines-hires-such-dedicated-people
[38]https://rauli.cbs.dk/index.php/jba/article/view/6132

When your company has the ability to *see* the human being for whom you're creating experiences, that sets you apart. That decidedly empathetic ability will never be achieved just by tracking clicks or charting sales trends. It can only be accomplished through a human to human connection. Doing this facilitates customer-centric decisions every step of the way and positions you to envision and create experiences that delight and support the people you serve.

Human insight is the missing dimension for many businesses competing in the Experience Economy. Read on to find out why this is the case, and how you can incorporate it into your business.

# CHAPTER 2

# The Missing Dimension

## Why and How Human Insight Powers Great Experiences

Throughout history, people have related to another by making interpersonal connections through stories.[1] We rely on multiple human signals to give us depth of comprehension: listening to someone speak, hearing their tone of voice, watching their facial expressions and body language, and observing their emotional reactions.[2]

This type of gut-level perception cannot be replaced by charts and graphs. It must be absorbed through observation and processed by an actual person, who then decides what it means and how to react to it.

Coaches cannot train athletes just by analyzing team statistics. They must watch their athletes play, talk to them, and build emotional

---

[1]https://time.com/5043166/storytelling-evolution/
[2]https://www.nbcnews.com/health/body-odd/eons-after-words-why-do-humans-still-need-body-language-flna873326

and cognitive understanding of each team member's needs and abilities before they can decide how to advise them.

Managers cannot oversee employees just by tracking hours logged or sales closed. They need context, critical circumstantial information that allows them to understand the fullness of an idea or event. They also need shared experiences and trust to see the full picture.

Without these added dimensions of understanding, any decisions they make will feel tone-deaf and misguided.

The same paradigm applies in business when companies explore customer perspectives.

Think about a digital team responsible for the checkout experience. Imagine them watching actual customers struggle to purchase a product online and listening to their frustrations. Observing those customers as they react to the clunky checkout process and hearing them explain what they *thought* would happen gives the team very different information than tracking clicks and abandon rates. It provides a more holistic understanding of where customers struggled and why, what they had expected but didn't find, and—most importantly—exactly what needs fixing.

Once the digital team members have spent time observing customers and gathering feedback, they have a better understanding of what it's like to *be* a customer. They can relate to customers' struggles and confusions, build a level of empathy that no other data source can provide, and make informed decisions to enhance the experience. *This is human insight in action.*

The beauty of gathering human insight is that it doesn't require giant sample sizes: Trends tend to emerge after talking to and observing just a handful of customers. Here's a scenario that will show you what we mean; imagine you're hanging out with a group of people and someone gets up to grab a drink or go to the bathroom. As they walk across the room, this person trips over a bump in the carpet. A few minutes later, someone else gets up to grab a snack and that person trips over the same bump in the carpet. You don't need everyone to trip over that bump to recognize you've got a problem, or even to start honing in on a solution. Smaller samples that are representative of your population can provide rich, narrative feedback to promote understanding of customer needs and pain points.

And to return to our hypothetical with the digital team, lacking this perspective means they're just placing bets on what to change and hope metrics move in the right direction. They're making educated guesses based on patterns they see in the data instead of acting on observed behaviors and genuine feedback. Some might argue that making and testing educated guesses is, essentially, the build-measure-learn protocol, but why not ensure your guesses are as educated as possible? Why not make well-informed, smarter decisions that increase your likelihood of success, ones that make you successful earlier, more often, and at a lower cost?

Here's a real world example.

AAA Club Alliance (ACA), one of the three largest AAA Clubs in the United States, knew with precision what customers were doing on its website, but they were unsure why potential customers were not completing the membership sign-up process. The various tools at ACA's disposal produced large quantities of data but little in the way of the insights they needed to understand how to improve this conversion rate. And despite rigorous analysis and targeted updates, these efforts failed to produce the desired results.

After connecting with real customers to gain human insight, they quickly learned that people were simply overwhelmed with information on their website. This insight not only explained why membership sign-up conversion rates were low, but also empowered AAA Club Alliance to streamline the experience by prioritizing information and making interactions informative, persuasive, and easy to navigate. After numerous design iterations with human insight informing the team along the way, they arrived at a solution that was significantly cleaner, more concise, and easier to use.

After these changes were live, ACA saw a 30 percent increase in overall conversions across all membership types, with a 55 percent lift in Premier Memberships, its highest tier of service. These improved conversion rates alone helped drive a remarkable 39 percent lift in member acquisition revenue.

After these key wins, the team saw wide adoption of human insight to continually learn and improve the member experience. Scott Lugar, the chief marketing officer at AAA Club Alliance, says human insight "empowers us all to make better decisions, and I'm never going back to the way we did things before. Having human insight at our fingertips has created a cultural shift in the way we iterate and innovate."

Human insight is the only way to know what it feels like to *be* your customer. And knowing that is the only way to continually create, design, and refine experiences that support and delight your customers and drive business success.

# Existing Customer Data Sources Don't Give Us the Full Picture

You can have near-endless supplies of data charting purchases, clicks, page views, even survey results and still fail to assemble a complete picture of your multidimensional, decidedly human customers. They have diverse lived experiences that will be masked by the numbers. They have complex psychologies that may influence choices in ways that data cannot capture. They have overlapping identities that are rich and difficult to understand. They're just too sophisticated to be boiled down into numbers.

Let's talk about the common types of customer data that teams use and why they fall short.

## CRMs Answer: "What Am I Doing with My Customer?"

Most businesses cannot function without these tools for managing customer information and relationships. CRMs like Salesforce and Zendesk are the systems of record and bodies of knowledge that underpin modern businesses.

The pitfall of these systems is that they only offer information about your customers from *your* perspective, so everything is viewed through the company lens—which is self-serving and the antithesis of customer-centricity.

## Analytics Tell You: "What Is My Customer Doing in My Product or with My Experience?"

This is observable customer activity, such as which stores are getting foot traffic, what individuals are buying, even some tidbits of general sentiment being expressed by your users and customers. Analytics is behavior seen at scale, which can help you identify patterns and areas to focus on.

However, extrapolating meaning from data patterns can be tricky. You run the risk of superimposing your ideas, logic, or even hopes and preferences on the data. You're making educated guesses about motivations and you might guess wrong.

## Surveys Tell You: "How Do They Feel About My Experience?"

The final tool in the customer data triumvirate is surveys, which can offer a bit more information about opinions and motivations than CRMs and analytics. Surveys provide access to prompted, anecdotal feedback from customers. That's a good start. It gives you a multi-dimensional impression of them as individuals, and a direct line to their recollections and impressions.

Unfortunately, surveys have the longest list of drawbacks. For starters, it's quite difficult to design a survey that's both objective and accurate, which means the data you get is likely distorted. Offering rewards or incentives, a common practice to capture more responses, may get you a higher response rate, but it may also skew your results.

Surveys are often sent *after* an experience has happened, which is troubling since more and more studies are proving that human memory is extremely unreliable.[3] Finally, there's survey fatigue, bots infiltrating online surveys, and the fact that people are apt to lie if they think doing so will benefit them.[4]

## Human Insight Tells You: "What Is It Like to Actually Be My Customer?"

This is frustrating. We get it. After all, we've got such sophisticated tools for understanding customers. And those tools remain essential, but *none* of these data sources will tell you, "What is it actually like to *be* my customer?"

---

[3]https://www.ncbi.nlm.nih.gov/pmc/articles/PMC4183265/
[4]https://www.ncbi.nlm.nih.gov/pmc/articles/PMC5639921/

None of them drill down deep enough to show you a customer's real and authentic perspective. None of them give you access to truly diverse viewpoints, or input from people with a wide variety of life experiences. None of them provide the depth of understanding needed to create experiences that enchant real, live people; make them fall head-over-heels in love with your company and your offerings; and secure their enduring loyalty. None of them give you human insight.

# Why Human Insight Should Be Included in How Companies Assess Their Experiences

Customer experiences may seem like fleeting, undefinable moments, but fortunately for businesses, they've been codified for us by the good folks at Harvard Business School.

In a landmark piece for *Harvard Business Review*, business consultants B. Joseph Pine II and James H. Gilmore wrote, "An experience occurs when a company intentionally uses services as the stage, and goods as props, to engage individual customers in a way that creates a memorable event. Commodities are fungible, goods tangible, services intangible, and experiences *memorable*."[5] In other words, customer experience is all about doing something so outstanding that you make your company, product, or service unforgettable.

---

[5]https://hbr.org/1998/07/welcome-to-the-experience-economy

Companies that actively evaluate their own user experiences sometimes assess themselves against Forrester's Three Es of Customer Experience: effectiveness, ease, and emotion.[6] This is a great approach, but human insight is typically *missing* from the assessment, and we think that's problematic. Let's take a closer look.

## Effectiveness: Does It Meet Customer Needs?

The primary concern under effectiveness is "Does it meet a customer's needs?" When people interact with a product or experience with a specific goal in mind, can they do what they set out to do?

Example: Let's think about online banking. A function that seldom fails and delivers quickly on its promise would be the funds transfer function through your bank's website or app. The functionality is (usually) always there, and you can rely on it to do what you need it to do.

Many companies believe they are measuring effectiveness by tracking behavioral data. Your bank can see how many transfers you've made, which gives them a fairly clear picture of how effective the transfer function is. Or does it?

What about those times you had to make multiple transfers because the dropdown options confused you or you accidentally sent $500 instead of $50? The actual transfer function worked perfectly, so based on the data everything is peachy, but does your customer have the same perception?

*Behavioral analytics don't give a detailed picture of effectiveness.*

---

[6] https://www.forrester.com/report/Answers+To+Common+Questions+About+Forresters+Customer+Experience+Index/RES127441

**FIGURE 2.1**   Effectiveness Shown with Big Data and Human Insight

## Ease: Is It Easy to Use?

When evaluating ease of use, companies are looking to make the experiences seamless, error-free, and intuitive.

Example: If we stick to online banking, PayPal offers both effectiveness and ease to most users. You can both send and receive funds, do so with individuals and businesses, and make most transactions happen in mere seconds without navigating through endless screens. The website and app are seamlessly integrated, so your experience is equally easy at your desktop or on your mobile phone.

Ease of modern offerings is often rated through surveys. Companies will ask users direct questions about their experiences to find out if they are easy to use. "Is this easy to use?" is a straightforward survey question so businesses assume they'll get straight answers. But do they?

What about the 63-year-old woodworker with an Etsy store who totally gets the PayPal web interface but sometimes gets confused about how to transfer funds from his PayPal account to his bank account? Or if he's prompted by a pop-up that disrupts him as he's working on a transfer, he may hit the first button he sees to close it. He might say that PayPal is "easy to use," but the team misses a valuable perspective that could help make the experience even better.

**FIGURE 2.2**    Ease Shown with Big Data and Human Insight

*Survey results don't give an accurate picture of ease.*

## Emotion: How Does It Make Me Feel?

Last but definitely not least, companies have recognized that they need to make an emotional connection with their customers to drive loyalty.

Example: Venmo's emoji-enabled app and casual-fun branding mean that this relative newcomer to the online banking scene combines effectiveness, ease, and emotion pretty darned well. Many people first learned about Venmo as the app to use to split a shared restaurant bill among friends and continue to associate it with emotionally rich personal memories and activities.

Most companies use Net Promoter Score ("On a scale from 0–10, how likely are you to recommend us to a friend or colleague?") or other surveys to capture emotional reactions, which enable them to gauge some of the baseline feelings people register while interacting with their brands or products.

But can emotions really be reflected in a rating scale question? If a person connects on a personal level to the brand or product but can't update their bank account information easily—and therefore would not recommend your product to a friend or colleague—does their response help you understand the full picture?

**FIGURE 2.3**   Emotion Shown with Big Data and Human Insight

*Satisfaction surveys don't fully capture the emotion an experience evokes.*

Our current methods of gathering information about our customers' experiences simply don't give us the depth of information we need. We need more detail, more nuance, and more truth from our customers than these methods can reasonably provide.

And perhaps most importantly, the information we get from the current methods for capturing the customer experience isn't actionable. Say a certain app gets three out of ten stars for ease of use from most customers or you see a rapid decline in engagement metrics. These shifts in key metrics tell you *what* is happening, but they provide zero context around *why* it's happening or guidance on how to address it.

So if the best customer experience always wins, and most businesses are hamstrung by their current tools for understanding customer experience, how do we pull authentic customer perspectives in to help us make smarter, better decisions?

# User Testing Leads to Human Insight

The best way to gather human insight is through user testing: asking people to talk aloud as they interact with and provide their perspective on products, services, brands, and the world around them. There are dozens of approaches to running user tests, some of which we'll explore in the coming chapters of this book, but all of them have some components in common.

All forms of user testing include:

- Observing (and sometimes conversing with) customers
- Listening to what they are saying and *how* they are saying it (sentiment, pace, intonation)
- Noting facial expression and body language

Some forms of user testing also include:

- A record of what customers are interacting with—a real world experience, a digital experience, or a combination of both—and *how* they are interacting with it.
- Additional context, such as the environment around them. For example, how their pantry is set up or what other apps besides yours they're using to manage their finances.

This collection of human signals—behaviors, body language, facial expressions, and verbal sentiment—provides a vivid, first-hand view of what it's like to *be* a customer, which is the dimension many teams are missing.

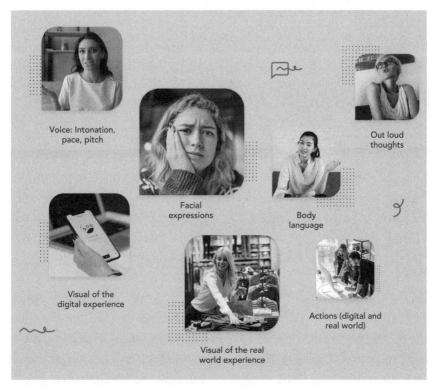

**FIGURE 2.4**  Human Insight Provides Multiple Human Signals

So, ideally, teams will approach the work of gathering human insight in this order:

1. **Execute user testing:** Observe customers as they interact with a product or offering or simply talk about their needs and challenges.
2. **Capture the session:** Create a record, usually in video format, of what happened when the customer interacted with a product along with their verbal feedback as they did so.
3. **Derive human insight:** Combine these human signals to deeply empathize and understand the customer's experience, their state of mind, and their actions.
4. **Share and take action:** Use this powerful human insight to build a shared understanding of your customers, to create new offerings, or to improve existing ones.
5. **Repeat:** Build this process into everything you do.

## Human Insight in Action

Without human insight, the heart of the company is the company itself, *not* the customer. With human insight in the mix, companies develop a more nuanced understanding of customer frustrations, dreams, and worldviews, which builds a level of customer empathy that you cannot get with charts and graphs alone. And when empathy for the customer can be cultivated and felt across business functions, everyone prioritizes stellar customer experiences.

Meal-kit delivery service HelloFresh models consistent cross-functional insight-sharing through their wildly popular "Insights Show." This event is the brainchild of James Villacci, Head of Global UX Research at HelloFresh, who knew that sharing curated videos of customers using the HelloFresh experience would be illuminating and transformative. To create a show, the UX Research team synthesize relevant recent learnings from across the company, compile them into fun and engaging "episodes," and regularly host meetings to share them out. Hundreds of HelloFresh employees attend and participate.

Though it wasn't always that way. When "The Insights Show," first started, it focused on a much smaller cross-section of work and drew just a handful of attendees per session. But word spread and the initiative gained traction, to the point that each member of the UX Research team hosted an "Insights Show" for their individual teams. Worried that this approach would keep insights siloed into isolated groups thereby defeating the purpose, the team transformed the presentation of these videos into company-wide events.

That's where "The Insights Show" blossomed, bringing attendees from multiple departments across the company, including product managers, designers, engineers, marketing experts, leadership, and operations staff. The show is structured to be highly interactive; the hosts will frequently pause the video to ask multiple choice questions such as, "What do you think the customer will do next?" The events build empathy and a shared understanding of customers that gets referenced in both meetings and casual conversation. Villacci says it's not uncommon to overhear someone saying, "Remember when we saw that happen at 'The Insights Show'?"

"They all want to learn," he explains. "And it's just a thirty-minute commitment."

The audience members of "The Insights Show" aren't always running user tests themselves, but they are eager to consume and apply their new learnings. Frequently, the show sparks related questions for attendees, which they're inspired to explore further.

On top of "The Insights Show," which captures and reflects a variety of customer opinions, HelloFresh encourages all of its employees to sign up for the service themselves. HelloFresh believes that when employees are able to have the same experience as customers, it builds understanding and empathy. They can literally put themselves in the shoes of the people they serve.

Integrating insight at every level has paid off for HelloFresh. The company is the market leader in a highly competitive space and has built a reputation as a genuinely customer-centric organization, due, in no small part, to continually bringing their customers to life through human insight.

# Why We Overlook or Dismiss Human Insight

So if human insight is the secret to building and supporting great experiences, why do so many teams overlook it?

Some key decision-makers have been conditioned to believe that numbers are all they need to make sound business decisions, and many of them don't realize what they're missing. Even though only 23 percent of initiatives driven by big data alone turn a profit,[7] few leaders are making the connection. They don't realize (yet) that seeing the world through their customers' eyes is an ability they need to drive real growth.

On top of that, many organizations have spent big bucks to create robust data collection and analysis machinery. Between sourcing, architecture, governance, and analysis, McKinsey estimates that a midsize institution with $5 billion of operating costs spends more

---

[7] https://www.capgemini.com/wp-content/uploads/2017/07/the_big_data_payoff-turning_big_data_into_business_value.pdf

than $250 million on data.[8] It can be hard to justify even more when you've invested that much in data management.

It can also be hard to convince companies that human insight collection can be done efficiently and effectively. Many executives assume it will take tons of time and money to get the input they need from real customers.

For example, we spoke with several leaders at a consumer packaged goods company who mentioned that they utilized "pantry audits" to understand customer preferences and buying patterns. Pantry audits are in-home visits where a team documents the contents of people's cupboards and interviews them about food shopping, consumption, storage, and organization habits. But the company we spoke with told us audits were a major pain to organize, time intensive, and so costly that they assumed they'd have to phase them out. That is, until we showed them we could get dozens of video-based pantry audits for them in just a few hours' time.

Last on the list of reasons why companies overlook human insight? Inertia. When faced with the choice to pull in customer perspectives that reflect the multidimensional nature of customers or just use existing data and long-held beliefs, many leaders choose the latter. It feels easier. It's faster. And if they've got smart, seasoned people on their teams, they may assume those people can ferret out the insights needed to spark growth. Can't internally generated ideas—ones based on meticulously collected customer data—do the heavy lifting?

The answer is no, of course not. Not without some input from real, live customers.

---

[8]https://www.mckinsey.com/business-functions/mckinsey-digital/our-insights/reducing-data-costs-without-jeopardizing-growth

# Human Insight for the Win

So, it's clear that human insight is critical. But many companies lament the lack of an efficient and scalable mechanism that really helps them understand the experience through the eyes of their customers. And they need it. Badly.

In the chapters to follow, we'll show you how to run user tests that are fast, affordable, and easy to implement across the enterprise. We'll explain exactly how and when to collect human insight and offer suggestions on how to weave it into the fabric of your organization.

You want to delight your customers with frictionless, valuable experiences that drive loyalty. And once you embrace human insight, you'll be able to do just that.

# PART 2

# The Solution: Human Insight Powers Customer-Centric Actions

**W**e believe that gathering human insight should be simple, but it should also be done thoughtfully, responsibly, and with the right intention. Given a few guidelines and parameters, anyone within your company should be able to set up a user test, observe and talk with customers, and draw savvy conclusions. With that in mind, we've packed this section of the book with advice, principles, and ground rules that everyone from seasoned execs to new hires can review and apply.

We start by helping you define and formulate the questions you need answered and urging you to give serious thought to which people should be consulted. (As we'll say many times, you are *not* your customer!) We explore the dangers of human bias and offer tips for circumventing it, and then dive into the many ways you can leverage your learnings to impact the customer experience and the business as a whole.

# CHAPTER 3

# What're You Trying to Answer?

## Mapping a User Test Approach to Your Desired Learnings

Getting meaningful, actionable, high-quality human insight from user testing is all about asking the right questions of the right people. We desperately want more businesses to seek and apply human insight, but we know from experience that asking misguided, unfocused, or badly formulated questions of your customers can be disastrous.

Remember in 2009 when Walmart surveyed their customers about store layout? The retail giant asked its shoppers what seemed like a straightforward, customer-centric question: "Would you like Walmart to be less cluttered?"

When the answer turned out to be a resounding "Yes!" leadership swung into action. Hoping to both declutter stores for current customers and potentially start attracting higher income Target shoppers in the process, they rolled out an initiative called Project Impact.

This five-year plan for streamlining stores, improving navigation, and upgrading interior aesthetics was ambitious and aggressive. Millions were spent replacing fixtures and renovating existing stores, but the most noticeable change was removing the merchandise that traditionally sat in the aisles between fixtures. To do this, the leaders of Project Impact had to remove nearly 15 percent of the items sold in physical Walmart stores.

Although initial customer survey responses to these changes were positive, the eventual results were catastrophic. Once the Project Impact renovations had transformed around 600 Walmart stores, it became clear that reducing store inventory was a mistake. Year over year same-store sales plummeted, and the project was put on indefinite pause. Walmart lost an estimated $1.85 billion in sales plus hundreds of millions they spent renovating the actual stores.[1]

All because they asked a poorly worded question.

We know that sounds ominous, but don't worry. We're going to show you exactly how to avoid misfires like Project Impact. And the key is carefully calibrating your questions *before* you ask them.

Here's how.

---

[1]https://retailzipline.com/blog/what-walmarts-cleanliness-experiment-teaches-about-customer-feedback/

# Understand How Your Question Relates to the Business

Curiosity is an important ingredient to better understand your customers, but product and marketing teams must be careful about letting it run wild in user testing. The user testing process is about finding answers to questions meant to improve the customer experience. That means formulating the approach with direct links to business outcomes so you can tie your experiments and findings to what matters most.

In practice, this means ensuring that your immediate questions around a campaign or product—the ones that rise to the surface naturally as you hone and develop—map back to high-level organizational goals.

For example, if you're responsible for the self-service experience for your company and notice that people are dropping off after viewing the FAQ section of your site, you'll want to know why so you can address it. That's the question at the testing level, but if you consider the next logical step up it would be the project, which could be something like a FAQ redesign. One level up from there is the larger initiative, which is your focus on improving the self-service experience. And finally, if you level up again, you've linked to the topline business driver, which is to reduce costs.

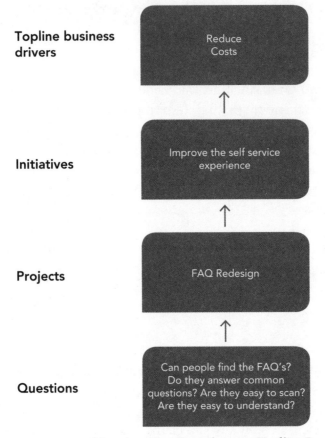

Topline business drivers — Reduce Costs

Initiatives — Improve the self service experience

Projects — FAQ Redesign

Questions — Can people find the FAQ's? Do they answer common questions? Are they easy to scan? Are they easy to understand?

**FIGURE 3.1** Mapping Your Question to a Topline Business Driver

And *that's* the level that C-suite execs will be eager to discuss.

To make their value clear to leaders, the questions asked of customers must ladder up to something that matters. You're using time and energy to explore it; it's an investment. Spend it wisely. Spend it on a question that will help you understand how to get to market faster, sell to new customers, drive customer loyalty, cut costs, or obliterate the competition through great customer experiences.

# Consider How and Where You Plan to Apply Your Learnings

The questions we formulate and ask of our customers don't just need to be tied to the business, they need to be tied to where you are in your workflow or development phase and how you plan to apply your learnings. For example, it's wildly inappropriate to ask about feature prioritization when you're still sussing out what customer problem you'll solve. Try not to get ahead of yourself. Instead stay grounded in the work you're doing right now.

Wondering what questions are appropriate for various stages of common workflows and processes? Here are our suggestions:

## Questions to Ask *Before* You Create

Since you're in the early phase of developing your product, offering, or new brand positioning, the questions you ask of your customers should help you develop the right approach. Input from real people is valuable at every stage of this process, but it's especially important here.

You've got a hypothesis about a pain point, problem, or need, but until you connect with some customers and pick their brains, you don't have enough context or deep understanding to act on that hypothesis. You *must* talk to people outside the company walls to understand it deeply so you can respond appropriately.

A consumer-packaged goods company recently modeled this important strategy with a CEO-led initiative to change single-use products to reduce waste. Instead of jumping to a solution right away, the packaging design team performed a series of user tests to better understand the problem they were trying to solve.

The tests started by connecting with people who were willing to show the team their bathroom supplies, including how and where they were stored. The team focused on drain cleaner to make sure they weren't gathering information that would prove too broad to be useful. Then, they formulated a series of questions including, "How often do you clean your drain? Do you do it only when the drain becomes clogged or regularly? Would you show us how you tackle this task? Where do you store the product you use to clean your drain?" They were able to find out how often drain cleaning products were needed and used, whether people bought large or small bottles to accommodate their storage capacity, and even if refillable drain cleaner would appeal to them.

By getting customer perspectives that provided a glimpse into their worlds, the team could solve a problem they understood intimately, and this helped them bring the best solution to market.

## Questions to Ask *While* You Create

Before narrowing to a specific solution or idea, it's time to vet different solution ideas and pick a path. You should be using divergent thinking, design thinking (see sidebar in this chapter for more details), or other exploratory methodologies to sketch out rough concepts. You're likely tinkering with multiple ideas, which means this is a *great* time to get some user input.

## Design Thinking

As the customer experience becomes more and more important as a competitive advantage, companies must adopt strategies that align their organizations around their customers' needs. One viable methodology for this approach is "design thinking."

The concept of design thinking has been around for decades with roots in the Hasso-Plattner Institute of Design at Stanford, which is also known as d.school, and many credit IDEO founder David Kelley for bringing the idea to the masses. He defines design thinking as, "... a human-centered approach to innovation that draws from the designer's toolkit to integrate the needs of people, the possibilities of technology, and the requirements for business success."

But design thinking isn't just for designers. Swap out "designer" for "product team," and you'll have an accurate description of what product teams strive for on a daily basis. Design thinking also doesn't have to be the only framework your team relies on. One of the biggest draws to this framework is its consistent focus on keeping the customer at the center of every decision in the development process.

Most design thinking involves five basic phases:

1. Empathize with your users
2. Define your users' needs, their problems, and your insights
3. Ideate by challenging assumptions and creating concepts for innovative solutions
4. Prototype solutions
5. Test solutions

*(continued)*

*(continued)*

**FIGURE 3.2** The Design Thinking Framework
*Source for Framework: IDEO*

Although the design thinking framework is often presented as a defined process, it's important to note that each stage can happen at any time, as often as needed. This is an iterative and non-linear process, meaning the design team continuously uses their results to review, question, and improve their initial assumptions, understandings, and results. The only stage we suggest is mandatory is the Empathize stage, as that will inform everything else your team does and ensure your customer remains at the center of every experience you create.

Without sufficient testing and user input during the solutioning phase, you run the risk of building a suboptimal solution. Take Juicero, an at-home cold-pressed juice device that cost $400 back in 2016 at the height of the juicing craze. Founded by Doug Evans, Juicero raised $120 million and counted respected VC firms among its backers, including KPCB and Google Ventures, and yet it failed spectacularly once on the market.

The inner works of the machine were overengineered, brimming with specialized custom-tooled parts, and yet it still failed to do the one thing it was designed to do: create juice. In a Bloomberg video review, it was shown that the Juicero-produced QR code-stamped fruit bags could be more easily juiced by squeezing them manually than feeding them into the machine. Adding insult to injury, the fruit bags had strictly timed lives, which meant a full bag could be rejected by the machine on "freshness" grounds after a short duration. Had the creators of Juicero run even a handful of user tests, they likely would have gotten an earful about these frustrating features and been able to course-correct. Alas, the product sat on shelves for just a year before the founder decided it was a lost cause.[2]

While exploring various ideas, we've seen some teams and companies build landing pages to get customer reactions on proposed products or offerings. They haven't built a product or a true prototype yet, but they've hosted a landing page on their site so it looks relatively "real" to customers offering input.

Marketing teams can get feedback on early ideas and concepts, too. For example, something as simple as a moodboard—a visual collage that reflects a creative direction and language choices—is a perfect candidate for user testing. Teams can create multiple boards to show to users and collect their input. Teams may offer several options and ask, "Which of these makes you think of our brand?" or "If each of these were a famous person, who would they be?" This exercise

---

[2]https://deadstartuptoys.com/product/juicero/

can provide insight that informs campaigns, specific messaging, and branding discussions.

Ultimately, this is an interim phase. And the best possible course of action is to get lots of feedback on the *array* of possible solutions you're considering, so you can hone in on the one that will be most successful at launch.

Once you've selected the right solution path, now it's all about building it the *right* way. Building prototypes of physical products, websites, and apps makes everything feel more real—for you and for the customers who user test it. It can be tough to remain objective when you run user tests this late in the game since you've invested so much time and effort in concepting and building your offering, but you need to remain open to honest feedback.

If you're a veteran product manager or marketer, you likely know that products do get pulled at this phase. If user testing reveals an issue or hiccup that's big enough to cause major concerns, entire designs may get scrapped. When they're pushed through to release despite known issues, disaster may follow.

For example, video conferencing service Zoom offers virtual backgrounds to its users, but in late 2020 people noticed that the algorithm running the backgrounds didn't register Black users' hair. Or sometimes their entire heads.[3] An issue this severe should have been caught and addressed long before release.

## Questions to Ask *After* You Launch

No offering is ever perfect. Regardless of how much you (or your customers) love a solution, there's always something that can be

---

[3]https://onezero.medium.com/zooms-virtual-background-feature-isn-t-built-for-black-faces-e0a97b591955

fixed or improved, which is why we encourage companies to continue gathering feedback and running user tests after the launch of a new experience. Continual optimization based on regular collection of human insight leads to the best experiences.

Again, it may seem like post-launch user testing is overkill, but we promise you it's not. Here's an example to prove it to you: A mortgage service provider choose to continually user test their flagship app once it was launched.

After several rounds of user tests, they discovered that there were parts of the application checklist that people found confusing. For example, after completing the checklist and clicking "Apply Now," people expected to be done providing information, but instead were surprised to find even more form fields they needed to fill out.

Based on these learnings, the team immediately took measures to better communicate all of the required steps in the application checklist.

Today, when all the steps in the application checklist have been completed, customers are presented with a "Congratulations!" page. It is now clearly conveyed that there is nothing else required and their application has been submitted for review.

To make sure the changes met and exceeded customers' overall satisfaction, the company measured the Net Promoter Score (NPS) of the app before and after making the changes to the process. Before the changes, the app's NPS was -43. After the changes, the app's NPS was 67—a more than 250 percent increase in customer satisfaction. Clearly, testing post-launch was a worthwhile endeavor.

# Don't Ask Leading Questions or Go in to "Prove" Your Hypothesis

There's a big difference between performing user testing to explore customer perspectives and doing it to confirm your own beliefs. If internal teams are convinced that their new offering is "the next big thing" and run user tests to "prove" their idea, the learnings will be misleading. The questions will lead customers toward the answers that the company wants and hopes to hear. For more best practices on conducting interviews, see the following sidebar.

## Best Practices for Conducting Interviews

A live interview should be more like a conversation than a job interview with a fixed set of questions. Instead, you want a general guide that includes ideas for follow up questions in places where you'll likely want to dig deeper. Keep these tips in mind while you're conducting your interviews:

### Keep it casual

Make your interview feel like a casual conversation. Start out by breaking the ice with something simple, such as "Thanks so much for coming in today. How was your weekend?" or something similar. Allow a little time for your participant to warm up before you jump into a single line of questioning or pursue a specific topic.

### Push through the initial awkwardness

Getting to know someone new almost always comes with a dash of uncomfortable silence, a stutter here and there, and questions that sound like they should be coming from a therapist. Here's the good news: Feeling a little awkward usually means you're on the right path. Don't get hung up on the discomfort. Proceed along the general script flow that you've prepared.

*(continued)*

*(continued)*

## Start broad

Ask for general information about an area of their life you're interested in, such as how they approach financial planning, before you jump into specifics such as what they think about 401k or mutual funds. If you get too specific too soon, you will narrow the conversation prematurely, bias responses, or both.

## Encourage the person to keep talking

A great way to keep your participants talking, without putting words in their mouths, is to simply acknowledge that you are listening with a casual "mhmm" or parrot back whatever they just said. For example, if they say, "I dunno, this page just looks weird...." you can wait a few seconds and then repeat what they said, "the page looks weird ..." and simply trail off without actually asking a question. This usually prompts them to complete their thoughts and also helps reinforce that you're actively listening to them.

## Take five

When you want to jump in to interject or interrupt anything your participant says or does, a good rule of thumb is to slowly count to five in your head. This technique gives you an easy measure to ensure you're not inadvertently cutting out valuable details.

Apologies to Walmart, but their question in the anecdote mentioned earlier ("Would you like Walmart to be less cluttered?") is a perfect example of one that nudges the respondent toward a particular answer. Even shoppers who hadn't given a single thought to the layout of stores might find themselves thinking, "Well, now that you mention it, yeah. Walmart *does* feel cluttered."

So how do you avoid biased questions? Here are some tips for you.

- **Avoid questions that require a yes or no response.** If you perform an exit poll and ask, "Did you enjoy your experience today?" you may inadvertently influence answers as people will likely just agree with you. A better way is to frame your question as, "Would you tell us about your experience today? What worked well? What didn't?" Or ask them to rate their experience on a scale.

- **Be careful with positive or negative framing.** Questions like "How delightful was your interaction with us today?" are framed in a positive light and will likely lead to favorable answers. In Walmart's case, "clutter" is a negative frame that was embedded in the question itself, and it certainly skewed the resulting data and sent the teams down a disastrous path.

- **Don't give away the answer in your question.** If you ask, "Have you spent at least $100 online in the past month?" you're pointing respondents toward the answer you want and expect. It's better to ask open-ended questions like, "How much have you spent online in the past month?"

## Keep It Focused

One of the biggest stumbling blocks we see when teams run user testing is that they cover too much ground. They decide to ask a myriad of questions in a single user test, such as:

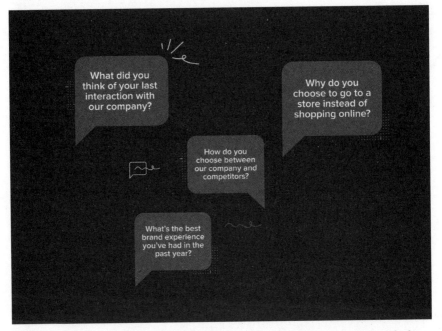

**FIGURE 3.3**   Too Many Broad Questions in a User Test Can Overwhelm

Questions that cover a wide range of topics in a single sitting yield answers that are more overwhelming than illuminating. And when you go too broad, it's exhausting for both the questioner and the questioned. Remember that you're not writing a thesis here. Keep the focus narrow, the question snackable, and have a clear line back to the business outcome at hand. And if you do need to cover a lot, consider breaking it up across multiple user test sessions. Three thirty-minute sessions, each focused on a specific topic, is a better approach than a single ninety-minute session that covers several meaty topics.

## Keep Your Question Top-of-Mind

Before you start gathering information, commit to holding yourself accountable to your question. User testing is fascinating and compelling work that tends to breed tangents and rabbit holes. Once you start asking your question of actual users and hearing their replies, you may want to start piling on related questions or see if you can quickly get their feedback on a more general matter. Don't.

Veering away from your original question will do two things:

## It Will Distract You

When you're coming up with your questions, do your best to consider possible distractions. Are there certain related ideas that you need to filter out? Are there aspects of the user test that are likely to yield the best signals and therefore merit more of your attention? Remind yourself of your narrowly focused and business-contingent question so you don't get distracted and charge off in some new direction.

For example, let's say your question is: "How do we differentiate from the competition?" As you begin to gather customer input, you may start wondering about the customer support experience your company provides, which leads you to ask customers about their thoughts on chatbots. Occasionally, this yields new initiatives that are more valuable than the original ones. More often, it eats up your time and resources while your carefully formulated question languishes unanswered.

## It Will Drown You

Adding more questions to the mix means generating more data to sift through. Sometimes much, much more data than you have the time or resources to examine. If you lose sight of your original question or add onto it, you'll be overwhelmed by the amount of information that comes back to you.

To illustrate, if your original question is "How do we clarify our pricing?" but you allow feedback on shipping options to sneak in, you've just doubled your scope. That second question is definitely related, but is it germane to your larger objective? More specifically, do you have the bandwidth to tabulate and analyze those auxiliary responses? And does the team have the capacity to make improvements to any issues you identify?

Once it's formulated, your question should become your beacon. Revisit it whenever you launch a new experiment, start working with a new panel of customers, or enter a new phase of development. Make it your mantra. Ensure it's with you at every step of the user testing journey.

# Ask Questions with the Intention of Sharing with Others

Plenty of the stories and perspectives you capture will only be relevant to you and your team, but the broad themes and learnings can and should be disseminated. With that in mind, consider including a handful of questions in your user test that will yield some intriguing and shareable perspectives. These shouldn't be the only questions you ask, obviously, but they can be part of your overall approach.

A few of our favorites include:

- **Use three words to describe how this experience makes you feel.** This is a great way to prompt customers to generalize and offer up language that can be repurposed into marketing efforts.
- **Describe this [value prop, product, company mission] in your own words.** This gives you a peek into how the customer's mind works and may also pinpoint areas of misunderstanding that can be proactively addressed.
- **Capture a few meaningful or important interactions to grab the interest of viewers.** Consider including activities

that will be compelling to watch and tie to business performance; think initial onboarding, downloading and installing an app, searching for information on your website, or reacting to an ad.

Socializing these customer perspectives creates universal buy-in and sharing snackable human insight ensures that team members across the organization understand the people they're serving.

# Always Ask Why

As we've mentioned, numeric data can give you tons of information about *what* people are doing, but it cannot tell you *why* they're doing it. Fortunately, running user tests gives you the opportunity to gather that perspective. Understanding customer motivations, complicating factors, and reasoning helps you craft offerings and experiences that truly serve them. Without this level of insight, your assumptions are driving the train.

Consider this example: You notice a trend of customers opting out of your text alert program, so you decide to investigate and send them a multiple choice survey. Even if the majority select, "I don't like getting texts from companies," you still haven't reached a true "why." If you interview customers directly, you may find that many of them have mobile phone plans that charge a fee whenever you ping them. Or maybe your texts arrive at inopportune times, such as when they're running a daily stand-up meeting or putting the kids down for a nap. In the case of irritating text fees, you could create a way to direct people opting out of texts toward signing up for email alerts instead. In the case of bad timing, you could offer customers the chance to select the time of day text alerts hit their phones. But if you never ask, and just stop at "I don't like getting texts from companies," you'll likely assume all of those people are lost causes and let them drift away instead of actively cultivating their loyalty.

The nature of this work is to do everything in your power to deeply understand the people you serve. If you're looking to get yes or no responses, there are other, more efficient ways to do that. User testing is about getting context, understanding motives, and digging into the "why" so you can make better business decisions.

# When You've Formulated a Decent Approach, Reuse It

Here's some good news: You can reuse many of the questions you formulate for future user tests. Save common questions and approaches so you can refer back to them. There's no need to start from zero every time you are planning a new user test. As you ask questions of customers more and regularly, you'll develop a trusted approach or template to make the process quicker and easier for future tests.

And now that you've got the tools you need to formulate and ask questions that yield insightful customer answers, you need to go out and start asking them. But *who* should you ask? And how can you find those people?

Keep reading to find out.

# CHAPTER 4

# You Are Not Your Customer

## How to Get Access to the Perspectives That Matter

I f you're not user testing with the right people, you'll capture misleading human insight.

Even if you've spent ages choosing and honing your question and you're *absolutely sure* it's been calibrated to prompt honest, helpful answers, you need to make sure you ask it of the right individuals and groups. Otherwise, the human insight you gather will lead you astray.

Here, let us prove it to you. In the 1950s, smooth-tasting Arabica coffee beans began to rise in price, in part because they were delicate and prone to dying under cold or inclement weather conditions. So, in 1954, Maxwell House, a popular brand of grocery store coffee, began blending Robusta beans into their mix to lower costs.

Not only are Robusta beans cheaper and more plentifully grown—they're pest and weather resistant.[1] Unfortunately, they taste bitter and harsh. To mitigate this issue, Maxwell House introduced Robusta slowly and gradually so customers could acclimate to the flavor. They performed user tests along the way, asking longtime drinkers of Maxwell House to weigh in, and virtually none of them noticed a difference between all-Arabica and Arabica cut with a hint of Robusta. So they continued to add more Robusta, test among loyal customers, and roll out blends with less and less Arabica.

For many years sales boomed and profits were healthy, but over the decades, sales began to decline. Maxwell House's U.S. market share in fresh and instant coffee sales fell from 8 percent in 2013 to 6.7 percent in 2019, and in April of 2019 parent company Kraft Heinz was attempting to sell off the once-iconic brand.[2] So what went wrong? Maxwell House consistently found that longtime customers were happy with their product. Weren't they doing everything right?

Not quite.

The company was only asking current customers for input, the people who had been slowly acclimating their palates to a Robusta-dominant blend. New customers who tried Maxwell House for the first time frequently hated it, so the company was failing to attract new buyers. Had they run user tests with both current and prospective customers, they may have avoided this mistake and saved their brand.[3]

---

[1]https://www.theatlantic.com/health/archive/2009/06/arabica-vs-robusta-no-contest/19780/

[2]https://nypost.com/2019/04/25/kraft-heinz-struggling-to-find-buyer-for-maxwell-house/

[3]https://shahmm.medium.com/how-market-research-failed-the-brands-a1fb04ca35a9

When you're planning a round of user testing, you can't invite just anyone to the party. And, surprisingly, you can't always just invite your current customers to weigh in either. Deciding who to consult to get the perspectives that matter to your company requires a thoughtful approach.

But don't worry, we're here to give you the inside scoop.

# You Are Not Your Customer

For starters, we're assuming you know who your current customers are or who you are targeting. And that you've spent some time and effort researching ideal markets and customer profiles for the new offering or updated product. There are entire books outlining methods for customer identification and validation, so we won't dig deep here.

Now, since you know who your current and ideal customers are, you must also know that *you* are not your customer. Right?

We're going to say it just one more time for emphasis: *You are not your customer.*

You may think you know this already and you may acknowledge it at the surface, but this critical mandate may not have penetrated deeply enough to protect you from risky assumptions. Far too many product managers and marketers assume their customers are "just like" them. Even worse, some think they can channel what their customers want and need, which often leads to ill-conceived products and miscalibrated messaging.

# Your Professional and Personal Networks Aren't Your Customers

Even looking beyond yourself into your immediate network isn't sufficient since many people have remarkably homogeneous professional and personal networks. Especially white people.

Recent polls show that 75 percent of white Americans have an entirely white network. By contrast, 65 percent of Black Americans report their network is entirely Black, and 46 percent of Hispanic Americans say their network is entirely Hispanic.[4]

This happens because we are drawn to people we believe will understand and accept us, so we gravitate toward people who we think are similar to us. Herminia Ibarra, a professor of organizational behavior at the London Business School, says, "Left to our own devices ... we produce networks that are 'just like me,' convenience networks."[5]

So you are not your customer, and your professional and personal networks aren't a trustworthy source for user testing-appropriate customers, either.

# The Patrons in Your Local Coffee Shop Aren't Your Customers

Even people in your immediate vicinity should be vetted before invited to give feedback on a prototype or marketing message.

[4]https://www.prri.org/research/poll-race-religion-politics-americans-social-networks/

[5]Devon Magliozzi, "Building Effective Networks: Nurturing Strategic Relationships, Especially for Women," The Clayman Institute for Gender Research, April 26, 2016, https://gender.stanford.edu/news-publications/gender-news/building-effective-networks-nurturing-strategic-relationships

If you work in Silicon Valley and ask people at a local coffee shop to react to it, there's a *really* good chance the people you interview will be fairly homogeneous. Now, if people in Silicon Valley are indeed your target audience, this is a fine approach, but most products and experiences don't target this very specific demographic.

Give careful thought to geographic concerns, especially if you're entering a new-to-you market. If your company is based in Singapore and you're hoping to launch a social media offering in the United States, you'll need to reach beyond American expats in your home city. Go the extra mile to perform user tests with current U.S. residents to ensure you deeply understand them so your solutions and messaging resonate.

So now you know who *not* to invite to your user tests. Let's dive into who you *should* be speaking to as you gather human insight.

# Who Are the Right People for Your User Test?

## They Have the Characteristics of Your Target Audience

First, start with the basic demographics. What geographic locations are you targeting? What age group are you targeting? If it's a B2B product, what roles or industries are important to you? Start by listing out all the basic information that unifies your target population.

Next, think about what is *unique* about your ideal customer. Do they spend a certain amount of money online each year? Do they manage their money with more than one financial institution? Do they have multiple children under the age of five?

Think beyond basic demographics details, like age and location—which are still vitally important to recruit for—and make sure you are filtering your potential participants for these more granular characteristics.

## There May Be More Than One Customer "Type"

You may have multiple customer types and that's OK. However, make sure you find people from each group when gathering customer perspectives.

For instance, if you're building technology that's related to K-12 education, you probably shouldn't just user test among students; you may need to gather human insight from parents, teachers, administrators, and perhaps even school board members.

Or if you're gathering feedback on a marketing campaign for first-time homebuyers, don't make the mistake of just conducting user tests for the primary earner in a two-person household; you'll want to speak to partners and also recruit some non-partnered individuals who are looking to buy.

In B2B contexts, you'll need to consider the question of "choosers versus users." Is the person buying your product or offering the same person who will be using it on a day-to-day basis? The head of IT might sign the purchase order, but will she be the one who installs the software on three dozen laptops? The person whose input you need if you're designing the product will be the end user, but you might want to get the chooser's thoughts as you're building your positioning.

## They Represent a Range of Your Target Audience

In addition to finding a range of demographics like age, location, and income, recruit diverse and inclusive audiences, including those who may be using assistive technology.

This is especially true for tech companies who may inadvertently default to certain levels of expertise and assumptions about access. Remember that some people have older phones or struggle to use mobile websites. Some folks don't have access to consistent or high-speed internet connections. Some parts of the world primarily use mobile phones when they go online and are therefore extremely reliant on mobile-friendly experiences.

As you begin seeking out users who will give feedback, do your very best to recruit a mix of people with a wide range of experiences. You're targeting a demographic, yes, but you still need diversity within that demographic.

For example, if you're building an alcohol delivery app and are targeting anyone over the age of twenty-one, don't just gather input from five affluent white people in their twenties and call it a wrap. Make sure you get a nice mix of ages, income levels, and ethnicities among all adults.

That said, your user group won't be perfectly balanced in every user test, and that's just fine. As you execute more user testing over time, you'll start to see *who else* you should include to get more comprehensive human insight. Like so much of business, this is an iterative process. Let your learnings compound over time. And diversify consistently to capture and analyze the contexts of your current and potential customers.

## They May Not Be Your Customer—Yet

You likely have a long, robust list of your current customers, which you can and should use for user testing. However, remember that your current customers can only tell you so much because they've already chosen you. (Remember Maxwell House!)

Additionally, current customers who are willing to give feedback tend to fall into two categories; they want to give feedback because they adore what you're already doing or they want to give feedback because they've got an axe to grind. They won't be an objective population. Valuable? Sure. But not objective.

# How to Connect with Your Perfect-Fit Users

So now that you have a sense of who to pull in for their perspectives, where and how do you find them? Here are some of the most commonly used approaches for recruiting user testing participants:

**Panel Companies** If you need to gather insights from an extremely specific or specialized group of people, a solid option is to work with a panel company or recruiting firm. These organizations often recruit participants and run user tests, but you can certainly do the testing and insight-gathering on your own and only rely on them for sourcing participants.

**Tech-Powered Panels** Online panels, like the Contributor Network provided by UserTesting, enable you to gather and run feedback sessions with people all over the globe. Since most capture the customer's voice, face, and the screens they're using, they offer the advantage of truly authentic footage.

**LinkedIn and Other Social Platforms** If you need a subset of professionals to provide input on a product or message, you can purchase targeted listings on LinkedIn. Another option: Create a post on other social media platforms to find the right people.

**Craigslist and Similar Forums**   Everyone from startups to enterprises has used Craigslist to find customers for user tests. When going this route, it's wise to send interested individuals through a rigorous screening process to vet that they are the right fit.

**Your Network, but Several Degrees Removed**   Since we just mentioned that you are not your customer and your colleagues are *also* not your customer, this may sound like a contradictory suggestion. But if you ask your network to ask the people in *their* networks, you may be able to drum up some good fits. This is especially true if you need, say, teachers or fitness instructors. Reach out to your friends and colleagues to see if *their* teachers or fitness instructors would consider participating in your user tests.

**Guerilla Intercepts**   As we mentioned earlier, gathering feedback from people in your immediate neighborhood without considering their demographics is a no-no. But if you have a customer profile and a good idea of where those people live, work, and play, you can show up there and do some on-the-spot user tests after you confirm they fit your profile.

**Live Intercepts on Digital**   Intercepting website or app visitors in real time can make for fast, high impact feedback. Although this often requires your IT or digital team to add code to your digital properties, it's a worthwhile investment if you want to recruit people who are truly engaging with you or your offering.

## Additional Tips for B2B Companies

B2B user testing has additional considerations, so here are a few tips for companies gathering human insight from business professionals.

**Customer Lists and Account Teams** Your sales and marketing teams likely have databases and email lists galore. Consider tapping into those, but only if those customers have opted in to be contacted by your company. Also, collaboration with the account teams before and after the outreach is necessary to keep everyone aligned.

**In-Product Intercepts** Similar to live intercepts on a website, the approach of recruiting people while they're in your product can be fruitful. Remember, these are the "users" of your product and not the "choosers" or buyers, so keep that in mind as you lean on them for feedback.

**Customer Support** Your support team talks to your customers all day, every day. And they have a lot to say. Establish relationships with your customer support team members so they can connect you to people who have feedback or product feature requests, but be sure to balance with feedback from those who aren't pinging support regularly.

# Do It Right—and Then Build and Manage a List

As with question formulation, there's no reason to start from scratch when looking for customers to include in a user test. It's worth your time to find the right individuals to ensure you get the right answers and a diverse spread of perspectives.

And if you take this approach, it will pay off later. No need to invest weeks or months recruiting every single time you need to perform user tests; the more you test, the longer your list of customers becomes, and the quicker you'll be able to launch new tests in the future. Keep in mind that the best practice is to cycle through that list of customers regularly and continue to add new people to it so you can consistently get fresh perspectives.

Organizations that can quickly gather critical customer perspectives and act on them have a distinct competitive advantage in our digitally transformed, fast-moving world. By cultivating a group of users who can provide reliable, insightful feedback on any customer-facing touchpoints, you'll make sure *your* company has that advantage.

# CHAPTER 5

# Capture and Analyze

## Sifting Through the Noise to Find the Signal

Let's say you've mocked up some visual designs for a new marketing campaign, sent them out to loyal customers for input, and just received a dozen recordings of user test sessions. This is exciting, right? With these videos queued up on your screen, you're about to dive into some honest feedback on your ideas.

Then you click "play," and an absolute avalanche of information comes tumbling out of your screen into your lap. In addition to the comments your users make and where they click, you're seeing body language and facial expressions that add nuance to what they're saying and doing. Tone of voice adds another layer to the opinions and feedback these individuals are sharing. It's a lot to process.

*Then* you realize that this user input isn't just overwhelming and totally subjective but is also passing through your own personal filters. As a person with specific lived experiences, you're only able to interpret these customer videos based on your unique viewpoint. This can get complex quickly ...

Don't worry, we've got your back. This chapter includes best practices for capturing and analyzing customer feedback all while mitigating bias. We will give you concrete steps and helpful guidance so you can mine those user test sessions for precious human insight.

But before we dig into all that, here's a quick (and fascinating) cautionary tale about the importance of approaching your analysis process with the right tools, team, and mindset.

# Bias Is Everywhere

Danish researcher and consultant Rolf Molich, a pioneer in the field of usability research, is constantly urging *anyone* who conducts user tests to acknowledge and find ways to counter their own bias. Back in 1998, he conducted a small study that confirmed that people administering user tests impact the results of those tests, no matter how carefully other variables are controlled.[1]

Molich's study—the first in his ongoing series of Comparative Usability Evaluation (CUE) investigations—revealed that bias impacts all user tests. And we mean *all* of it.

That first CUE study had four teams of UX researchers each independently conduct a user test of a calendar program, Task Timer for Windows. Each team was given the same instructions and tools, and they were all asked to report their findings in the same way. However, each team interpreted the instructions in different ways and conducted the experiments with slight variations. And, of course, they all got different results.

The four teams conducting user tests on the Windows calendar program reported a total of 162 problems, but only 13 of those

---

[1]https://www.dialogdesign.dk/cue-studies/

problems were found by more than one team.[2] Not much overlap. And proof that when it comes to user testing, we aren't guaranteed an iron-clad set of consistent findings.

This is no one's fault. Bias is a natural byproduct of being human, but it's definitely something we need to be aware of and combat.

Molich has continued to run CUE studies to investigate the reproducibility of user test evaluations and has made many overarching suggestions to get to insight and action that are as useful and as bias-free as possible. Here are his top recommendations for evaluating user tests that yield valuable and reliable results:

- **Have more than one person independently analyze user test sessions.** With more than one person involved in observing, more problems are detected and the observers get an opportunity to reflect and align together.
- **Consult people with local or domain knowledge to avoid uncertainty around what the participant is doing or commenting on.** These specific types of knowledge may be needed to interpret whether participants approach an activity appropriately, miss important information, or ultimately arrive at the right place.
- **Involve others when grouping and prioritizing uncovered issues**. This will likely reduce the number of highly rated problems and thereby help the team focus on what's most important.
- **Remove the "moderator" from the user test.** Due to the evaluator effect that occurs in user tests with a moderator, this approach appears to be a cost-effective alternative or supplement. Some technology-powered human insight platforms, such as UserTesting, provide this option.

---

[2]http://www.dialogdesign.dk/tekster/cue1/cue1paper.pdf

- **Remember that perfection is not required in order for user testing to be worthwhile.**[3] The goal of user testing is to learn something meaningful that you can apply to the experience, and then test again.

So now you know that you will inevitably impact your user tests. Next up: How *the users themselves* may inadvertently skew what you find and what to do about it.

# Our Fallible Human Customers

If you've conducted any surveys or collected "self-reported" customer feedback and compared it to data that shows customer behavior, you've probably encountered the central truth of this work: What people *say* is often totally different from what they *do*.

If you are testing a sign-up page for your email newsletter and observing people work their way through the process, they may struggle in multiple spots and even articulate significant blockers, yet *still* report that the experience was a good one.

At least, they will if you ask them directly.

You might say, "How did you feel about the sign-up process? Did you successfully get your email into our system?"

And even if you know for a fact that they weren't able to sign up, they may say, "Oh, it was super easy! And yeah, I'm sure I'm signed up now."

They're not lying, per se. They're just telling you what they think you want to hear. This phenomenon is called social-desirability bias, and it shows up on surveys as well as in other ways to gather

---

[3]https://www.dialogdesign.dk/cue-9/

customer understanding. Put simply, it's the tendency of participants or respondents to answer questions in a manner that will be viewed favorably by others.[4]

It might mean over-reporting "good behavior" or under-reporting "bad behavior," or it might just mean telling the person collecting the feedback what you think is the "right" answer.

It's an unconscious response, something people do without even realizing they're doing it. But it does impact the results and ultimately, the action you do or do not take. (One workaround is to ask customers to talk to each other, instead of to you. See this chapter's sidebar, "Embracing Eavesdropping," for details.)

---

## Embracing "Eavesdropping"

Gathering human insight through user testing is a fantastic way to better understand your customers, but it's certainly not the only way. Motivate Design CEO Mona Patel has designed a process called "Insider Insight™" that leverages voluntary, one-on-one conversations to unlock what customers who know each other feel comfortable telling each other—and then that conversation is sent to the team to review and unpack insight. It often surfaces issues that people care about in ways that aren't possible in a traditional user test context with a customer and a moderator.

In Patel's own words, "Insider Insight™ leans into the ad hoc, off-the-cuff, back-and-forth of opinion, curiosity, and challenge that can only exist within strong relationships. It provides a way for businesses to get under the skin of a topic in the way that only people who know each other can."

---

*(continued)*

[4]https://methods.sagepub.com/reference/encyclopedia-of-survey-research-methods/n537.xml

*(continued)*

> This unstructured approach is not designed to replace traditional interviewing, user testing, or ethnographic research. It's just another dimension. Aside from the benefit of access to personal conversations, the method may be a viable option for cases where the time and budgets are tight. That said, there are specific skills required to process and sort through unfiltered narratives, but Insider Insight™ can provide valuable perspective into customer thought processes, beliefs, and priorities that complement other efforts to understand customer motivations.

It's also worth noting that people in user tests may be *more* engaged with your offering than they might be in normal life. They're concentrating harder, trying their best, and less likely to get distracted by other factors when they know their feedback is being captured or they are being observed. The level of focus that customers apply to user tests will exceed what they can give to your offerings when they're at home with kids who are demanding snacks, phones buzzing with text alerts, and the delivery person ringing the doorbell.

Now, don't despair. We're telling you all this to underline that user testing—especially the process of extracting meaning from these valuable customer perspectives—is an art, not a science. And you will become better at mitigating these unavoidable issues the more you do it.

It's important that you collect feedback often and maintain a learner's mindset in each iteration. It's also important to coordinate with observant teammates. Everyone on your team will bring a different perspective to the table and help you see the big picture. And it's *extremely* important to invite stakeholders from a variety of backgrounds to help with analysis so you can pool ideas, viewpoints, and institutional knowledge. (See the following sidebar for basics on running a user test.)

## The Basics of Running User Tests

Although user tests can take a variety of formats and be run in multiple ways, there are some common elements that they all share. In order to make them effective at generating human insight—and to ensure the participants know exactly what's happening and what's expected of them—we recommend these steps:

### Step 1: Introduce yourself and the purpose of the session

Warm up by introducing yourself and the goals of the session, which is to test the experience. This is a great time to underline that you are not testing *them*, just the experience. Nothing they do or say will be wrong, and no letter grades will be handed out at the end. You're hoping to collect input, feedback, and insights. Also, avoid telling them too much about the project or your personal investment in it; if you do so, they may feel reluctant to offer critical feedback during the session.

### Step 2: Explain what you'd like them to do

Give them a rundown of the session. Explain that you'll be giving them some activities to try using the experience you're testing, and that you'd like them to "narrate" what they're doing and what they're thinking as they do it. Consider demonstrating this for them; most people aren't used to describing their thoughts aloud, and modeling the behavior can be incredibly helpful.

### Step 3: Describe your role

It's important that they understand your role after you set up the session. Up until this point, you've likely been leading the conversation, but you will take the backseat once the session actually begins. Let them know that you'll be watching and observing and you may ask some questions along the way, but for the most part, you'll be silent. Of course, if something comes up during an activity and you want to ask for additional details, you're free to do so, but leave the

*(continued)*

*(continued)*

questions that require more thoughtful responses for when they've completed all the activities.

### Step 4: Wrap-up

Once they've completed the activities and you're through asking any follow-up questions, let your customers know how grateful you are for their help and participation, and invite them to come back again if they'd like.

# Three Key Human Signals When Sifting Through Your User Tests

The actual process of reviewing recordings, notes, or videos of user tests can be tackled in a variety of ways. How you process your user tests will depend on the question you are trying to answer and how you receive the data, as well as your timeline, tools, and team member availability. But regardless of your approach, the review and analysis process should always involve looking for the following three human signals.

## Signal #1: What People Are Doing and How They're Doing It

Imagine your user test involves gathering feedback on a new digital bathroom scale that pairs with a smartphone app and allows users to customize its settings and track trends in their weight. The tests you've designed capture information about how users interact with both the scale and the app, and your team is hoping to eliminate bugs, friction, and design flaws after a few rounds of user tests have been conducted.

The first round of video tests you and your teammates review show that users struggled with a variety of issues around turning on the scale, calibrating it, finding the app in the store, and creating an account, but most were able to complete all the activities. . . eventually.

- **How you might interpret this:** Success! The vast majority of people accomplished what was necessary to get both the scale and app working!

- **How you should interpret this:** That many hiccups is significant, even if users were able to complete the tasks after a prolonged struggle. They did what needed to be done, but would they want to do it again in that same way? Was it easy? Frictionless? When it comes to this human signal, it's vital to watch for frustration, confusion, inefficiency, and missteps instead of just assuming successfully doing what they were asked to do is all that matters. These friction points are the exact things you'll need to address to improve your experience.

## Signal #2: What People Are Saying and How They're Saying It

In two different videos, users who tested the scale said, "This is interesting" while examining features of the scale itself or the app.

- **How you might interpret this:** The user is engaged and finds the design to be attention-grabbing.

- **How you should interpret this:** The word "interesting" could mean at least a half-dozen different things. This is a case where what's being said and how it's being said are equally important. What aspect of the interface or product drew this comment? Was this a polite way of saying that something they encountered seemed weird or was it a genuine expression of interest? If possible, ask a follow-up question to clarify exactly what the user meant so you can take the right next step.

## Signal #3: Additional Contextual Signals

These include tone of voice, body language, facial expressions, and anything else you can observe outside of what users are saying aloud or doing with your offering. Let's imagine that several of your user videos show people leaning forward to get a closer look at the screen of the scale app.

- **How you might interpret this:** Users are engaged and excited!
- **How you should interpret this:** This action could definitely indicate engagement, but it might also mean that users are having trouble reading or understanding what's on the screen in front of them. Are they squinting? Smiling? Muttering under their breath as they attempt to connect the scale to the app? Try to determine if this is a positive or negative response based on contextual clues and if you're still in doubt, ask a follow-up question.

# What Does It All Mean and Where Do We Go from Here?

As you might have guessed by now, reviewing user tests will throw a whole bunch of data at you. You and your team must do your best to piece all of these inputs together. Examine them individually and as a whole, and pool your mental resources to land on the most reliable explanations. Investing this time and energy is worthwhile as it will drive your actions and decisions.

Start by acknowledging that truly "right" and utterly infallible answers are unlikely to emerge from this work. Your aim is to identify patterns, hone in on meaning and signals, and do something meaningful with the feedback. If you expect to surface unquestionably correct conclusions, you're just setting yourself up to fail. That said, there are a few trusted strategies for sorting significant insights from less meaningful ones.

The main one is frequency. *How many people experienced the same problem?* If one user complains bitterly about being unable to find the digital scale app in the app store but no one else struggles to locate it, that's worth noting but perhaps not actioning. If most users have the same feedback, that's meaningful and likely worth addressing. (Remember the "tripping over the carpet" scenario from Chapter 2? Just one tripper may mean you have a clumsy friend, but two or more underline a shared issue.)

In addition to asking yourself, "How many people experienced this?", consider the impact presented by a discovered issue. Let's say the users you tested were asked to register their digital scales on the company website, and most of them skipped this step until they realized it was critical to pairing the scale with the app. That may have caused minor inconvenience, but it didn't throw them entirely off course. If it sparked lots of vocal complaints or visible discomfort, it might have merited addressing. If not, weigh the true impact and decide if other concerns are more pressing.

Finally, consider any potential problems through the lens of persistence. If a particular issue comes up repeatedly within the same user test session—the scale fails to calibrate over and over again—that's meaningful. Pervasive problems are the ones that demand immediate response.

One of the best ways to sort through and prioritize your observations while keeping all three of these components in mind is to do some affinity diagramming with your team. (See the following sidebar for details on how to use this tried-and-true method for finding and prioritizing patterns and themes.)

# Finding Meaning Through Affinity Diagramming

One of the most widely used and trusted methods for helping teams collaboratively identify and prioritize experience-related issues is affinity diagramming. This process allows groups of people to organize data into clusters or themes based on their relationships, and vote on priority, which makes it easier for the team to align on next steps. Here's how it works:

**Step 1: Generate sticky notes.** While observing a user test, team members write down observations on sticky notes. One observation per note.

**Step 2: Group ideas.** Once testing is complete, team members gather with their sticky notes, which are placed on a wall or a (digital) whiteboard. Each note gets placed near "like" items and the team then creates themes or categories based on these groupings. So, for instance, you might end up with categories like content, registration, and navigation.

**Step 3: Prioritize.** Once grouped, everyone gets a set number of "votes" (usually between three and five) and they "vote" on the issues or themes with the highest priority. The ones with the most votes should be the ones that get addressed first, while the rest form a queue of issues for later on.

**Step 4: Identify issues to address.** For each "high" priority issue identified by the team, decide on effort to address and impact on the customer experience. By identifying which tasks have the highest impact and are the easiest to knock out quickly, the team can agree on next steps.

*(continued)*

*(continued)*

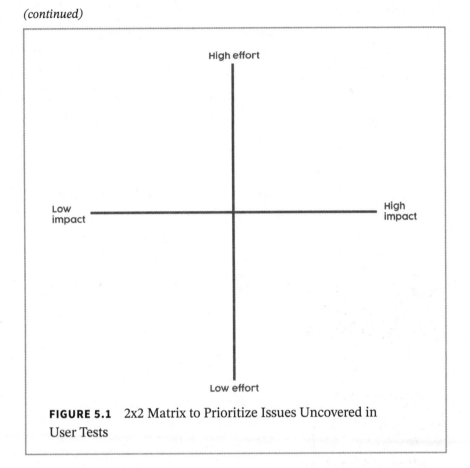

**FIGURE 5.1**   2x2 Matrix to Prioritize Issues Uncovered in User Tests

Discussing your findings in terms of frequency, impact, and persistence will help you process what you've heard and seen in your user tests. But what about the suggestions that helpful customers offer during or after they've completed the tests? If someone is engaged enough to recommend that you change the background color on your website or consider a different adjective in your headline, isn't that an actionable, customer-driven change you should implement?

Maybe. But our advice for teams is to consider these customer suggestions as a group and discuss their meaning, *never* to execute them as given.

More often than not, customers offer ideas based on surface-level concerns without accounting for design considerations or strategies that only internal team members will understand. Your job is to interpret the underlying problem that a customer is signaling through their experience or narrative, and solve *that*. Making the exact changes they want seldom addresses the root cause of their problem. (Even if they think it will!)

# CHAPTER 6

# Take Action on Human Insight

## Decide Where and How to Apply Your Learnings

When user tests surface an issue that needs to be addressed, that's human insight—and great guidance. Remember, this is the value that user testing provides. But that value is squandered if the insight you've uncovered isn't used to improve the experience you create for customers. Gathering human insight is the mandatory first step, but putting it to work is the equally crucial follow-up action.

One of the best places to start is deciding if you need to funnel this information to a different team or if you can address it yourself. Then identify the most actionable next step that will move it toward resolution or improvement.

There are a variety of issues and potential actions that arise as a result of user testing, and there is never a "right" answer on how to respond.

In fact, most problems that users encounter have multiple possible fixes. Here are some examples:

- If the feedback you received was that users needed more information, identify what needs to be added and integrate it. This may involve more or different imagery, more copy, or access to customer reviews.
- If the challenge that arose was related to struggles in finding something specific, you may have issues with your naming conventions, how you've organized your content, or even your search functionality.
- If you tested a marketing message or strategy and it fell flat, you may have a variety of issues to address, including tone of voice, visuals, or calls to action.

You get the idea. There's never a silver bullet solution when you've uncovered an issue. However, you do have to be open to trying different things, not getting stuck, and user testing again to see if you've made progress. It can be disheartening to get negative feedback from your customers, but you can't let it stop you in your tracks. Iterate quickly, ask for more feedback, and continue to optimize.

Deciding where and how to apply your learnings will depend on the level and type of feedback you get, but the bottom line is: *The human insight you collect is only valuable if it is used to improve the experience.*

# The Types of Human Insight You'll Get from User Testing

Let's explore some of the most common types of human insight teams get from user testing, and how to use them in the most productive ways possible.

## People Struggle to Use Your Offering: *"This Doesn't Work the Way I Think It Should."*

Nearly all teams who perform user tests unearth issues with comprehension, ease of use, interaction, navigation, and/or findability. Most of these challenges stem from design and copy issues that cause confusion. Plenty are minor and relatively easy to address, and a handful might have user-generated work-arounds.

Say your customers are trying to sign up for a new car insurance plan online and are confused about what the coverage includes, but they use chat or call customer service to get the necessary details to convert. That's a content issue. You could ignore it and let them continue to use their hack, but adding more detail to the website would make their experience easier and reduce your call center support costs.

Similar problems arise in the world of physical design, too. If you've created an airline check-in kiosk with a touchscreen and your customers want to check their bags but can't figure out how to activate the screen, they may go to the ticketing counter to deal with it. The desired activity has been completed, but it likely wasn't very enjoyable, efficient, or cheap. This design issue can be resolved with clearer instructions or a more sensitive touch screen.

There are also some UX-related problems that are more catastrophic in nature; these can cause customers to give up and go elsewhere. In the realm of content, if your shipping fees aren't clear in a checkout process and people abandon the experience, that's a serious issue. In store design, if customers need to address an issue at the service desk but they can't find it or the line is twenty people deep and they leave the store, you've put customer loyalty at risk. These user struggles—the ones that end in sheer frustration and giving up—should make you sit up and pay attention.

But the fact is that everything in this category typically has a clear and straightforward fix. You haven't misunderstood your customer or market entirely, you've just made a miscalculation, delivered a poor design, or omitted some key piece of information. The solves may be on the costly side, but the action needed to address them should be straightforward: add text, rearrange elements, tweak structure, do whatever it takes to change the content or design so your customers can do what they need to do without a hitch.

It's worth noting that these minor-seeming fixes are always worth addressing. In fact, they can have an enormous negative impact on the business if they go unresolved, especially if there are many of them littered throughout an experience. Just because customers generate hacks and work-arounds that get them to the finish line doesn't mean they'll get there happy and eager to run the same gauntlet again. If you don't optimize, you won't improve customer experience. And if your customer experience is dreadful, your customer may go elsewhere. Fix ease of use issues to differentiate yourself.

## People Are on the Fence About Your Offering: *"Is This Thing Really for Me?"*

In an independent study we did on the ASOS app, the UserTesting team was able to gather feedback on a website intro loop. It was a bright and action-packed carousel of video clips showing people in colorful clothing skateboarding, laughing, running, and other invigorating activities.

Some users loved it, but others expressed hesitation. They didn't loathe it, they weren't offended by it, but they were unsure. One contributor said, "I'm thirty-two, and I kind of feel a little bit too old for this. I don't know whether I am. That is my overall first impression. I love how it's not lagging at all. I mean, this is quite intensive. It's just a video nonstop."

Just as users can create workarounds and complete tasks despite ease of use issues, they can continue to use your website or products even if they feel hesitation. Even if they wonder, "Is this really *for me*?" But they may also get turned off and leave, or look elsewhere for options that feel more authentic to them. Do you want to risk that?

This type of feedback requires some repositioning or tweaking of how you present your offering. When this type of feedback arises, dig deeper so you can understand what isn't resonating and why. Ask them to describe what aspects of your offering feel clunky or unnatural to them, and try to get them to articulate why they're having negative reactions. This will help you learn the language they're using to express their preferences, and also give you a peek into their thought patterns and reasoning methods. With this feedback in-hand, you can adjust and tweak to meet their needs, then run another round of tests to make sure your offering is better aligned.

## People Don't See Value in an Offering: *"This Is Not for Me."*

This is the nightmare. Foundational, disruptive issues like this arise when you've fundamentally misunderstood your customer, your customer's problem, or the best way to solve your customer's problem. This happens when people don't connect with or see any value in what you're showing them.

For example, did you build an app for managing student loan debt and user test it to make sure people could download it, use it, and register for the service ... but never ask if they actually wanted the app in the first place?

If you've truly missed the mark, you're likely to know pretty quickly, but just in case you're unsure, here are some signals that people are finding little to no value in your offering:

- If you perform a user test in which you ask for three words that describe your offering and get replies like "not for me" or "don't need this".

- If you're asking for input on design or aesthetics and users are puzzled, say they're overwhelmed, or reject a concept immediately.

- If a marketing message doesn't resonate, and you get a clear negative response paired with other cues: grimacing, overwhelmed and so on.

- If you see a trend of nonresonance within your target audience, such as most people expressing the same level of displeasure or disapproval.

Hopefully it won't come to this, but misfires *do* happen. So let's talk about how to cope if one happens to you.

Start by returning to the beginning, where you were working to understand the problem and the customer as deeply as possible. We know, this is frustrating, but it's necessary in this case since the solution you created is being rejected by the very people it was designed for.

As you revisit your ideal customer profile and your problem statement, try to pinpoint where you took a wrong turn. Were you making the wrong assumptions? Did you choose a direction for your solution based on your own preferences instead of the customers'? Retrace your steps to find the source of misalignment.

Then commit to user testing early and often so you can course-correct as you refine.

# Build a Shared Understanding Through User Testing

Another aspect of taking action on user tests is socializing your results. Human insight gleaned through user testing is relevant to everyone who touches your product or offering, so be sure to share what you've learned. Here are some ways to do this:

- **Storytelling through videos of user tests:** Nothing is more powerful than seeing the world as your customer sees it. Most user tests include compelling or meaningful moments that can be used to tell a story of what happened while they had an experience and what they thought about it.

- **Ongoing socialization and sharing:** Keep the customer top of mind for everyone. Start meetings with a video clip from a user test showing customers talking about your offering so you can build up institutional knowledge across the company. Create a Slack channel to share interesting customer perspectives. Find ways to insert the voice of your customer into each and every day.

- **Pair metrics with customer narratives:** Using a video clip of a user test or even a customer quote to accompany key metrics—like engagement stats and conversion rates—can bring a whole new level of understanding to the team.

- **Get creative with presenting human insight:** Create interesting visuals to represent compelling data and findings from your user tests. For example, a word cloud can be used to communicate the words people commonly used to describe the offering or to show a difference in opinions.

# Tracking Learnings Over Time

Tracking and sharing your learnings also ensures that the body of knowledge you're accumulating can be used to build institutional knowledge and applied to *future* endeavors. As you continue to perform user tests over time, you'll cultivate a deeper level of understanding and connection with your customer. You won't just glimpse into their minds and hearts momentarily, you'll build up knowledge and insight that you can apply continuously.

Don't just learn about your users once, then trash or abandon your learnings. Be thoughtful about leveraging the insights they've given you again and again, over time and across offerings, so you can serve them better and build a shared understanding internally.

# PART 3

# The Playbook: How Human Insight Fits into Your Business

N ow that you've learned how transformative it can be to see through the eyes of your customers, and how to ensure the user tests you run will net you the human insight you need to make savvy decisions, it's time to talk tactics: How do you apply this to your day-to-day?

We've broken this playbook into three parts based on the teams most likely to run user tests: we have a chapter for product teams, a chapter for marketing teams, and a chapter for teams supporting the holistic customer journey.

However, if you're a product developer, you'll find plenty of interest in the chapter for marketing teams, and if you're a marketer responsible for demand generation, you'll learn a ton from the chapters geared towards product teams and the teams that support the ongoing customer journey. If you're an executive, a web developer, or a designer, just read all three. Trust us.

# CHAPTER 7

# Product Development

## Creating Products People Love

Apple, Uber, Netflix, Robinhood, Zoom, Tesla, Airbnb. All of these companies are industry disruptors that didn't just improve on existing offerings, they *created entirely new markets* with their radical innovations. It's no wonder they're widely revered and constantly cited as inspiration for everything from company mission statements to packaging to the design of digital and physical products.

But too many companies—and product development teams within those companies—claim they want to be "the next Uber" or "the next Airbnb" without committing to the mindsets and methods that made those companies into revolution-spawning market-creators. They did it by looking far beyond ease-of-use and clever design and forcing themselves to focus on solving key problems in new, groundbreaking ways. They did it by looking outside themselves and ensuring they were deeply and constantly attuned to customer pain points, frustrations, and preferences.

Unfortunately, it can be challenging to attune yourself to customer preferences because people don't always know what they want until you show them. Don't take our word for it: Jeff Bezos—perhaps the world's most influential disruptor—famously said in his 2016 shareholder letter, "No customer ever asked Amazon to create the Prime membership program, but it sure turns out they wanted it."

If you really want to be the next market-creator, consider Bezos' point. It's up to you to observe, listen, process, and boil down customer feedback and perspectives until you understand the core of the problem. Then you must find a way to solve it, iterate on that solution, keep gathering feedback, and ensure your solution delivers the absolute best possible customer experience.

And you must be willing to do this at multiple points in the product development process—not just right before it's released in an effort to "validate" it.

# Human Insight for Product Development

We know that product teams frequently follow predetermined workflows that repeat on a regular cycle. User testing can and should be incorporated into those workflows so product teams get steady feedback to learn, improve, and iterate every step of the way.

Jen Cardello, an insights leader with more than twenty years of experience optimizing human-centered design processes, has created a model for successful product development that's simple, elegant, and

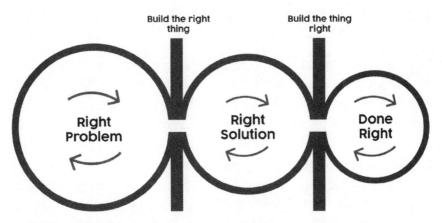

**FIGURE 7.1**    Jen Cardello's Product Development Framework
*Source: https://medium.com/fidelity-design/how-a-product-design-framework-guides-ux-research-de0e371384e9*

incredibly effective in getting teams to incorporate the customer perspective continuously.

We love this model because it urges product teams to consider the question of "rightness" at every turn, including:

- **Solving the *right* problem:** When understanding the problem space, what problem offers the "best" opportunity?
- **Building the *right* solution:** When sorting through possible solutions, what one is the most effective (as opposed to the easiest, cheapest, or quickest to leverage given existing company systems and resources)?
- **Building the solution *right*:** When refining the chosen solution, does it meet customer expectations or are you pushing it through to meet arbitrary deadlines?

In the following section, we cover the importance of each phase, share a related case study, and offer a recommended user testing approach you can apply today.

# Solving the Right Problem

**Why Is This Important?** Identifying and deeply understanding a problem set is arguably the most critical part of launching a successful product. Solve the wrong problem and you fail. Solve the right problem with the wrong solution and you also fail.

Understanding people's thoughts, perceptions, and feelings around an activity or event can help you identify gaps in an experience, and ultimately lead you to a compelling and valuable problem to solve. And you can do this in two key ways. First, by interviewing and talking to customers and second, by observing them as they interact with the world around them, including existing solutions or other contextual information.

From understanding a customer's pantry organization, office setup, or even where they place their smart speakers, this twofold method allows you to enter your customers' world and absorb information about how they think *and* how they behave.

Finally, if you believe you've identified a problem worth solving, it's important to validate that belief with your potential customers.

The interesting thing about choosing the right problem to solve is that you will likely uncover multiple worthy problems, and be forced to pick one. There are frameworks for identifying the best problem to solve. (See the following sidebar in this chapter for more details.) Once you've made your choice, you'll also have to gain a deep, contextual understanding of your chosen problem. Otherwise, you will start solving for a written description of a problem or a set of requirements without truly understanding the core need.

## Outcome-Driven Innovation

Some companies use frameworks like the Outcome-Driven Innovation (ODI) model to guide thinking at this phase. It asks teams to lead not with their own internally generated ideas, but instead to investigate and design for unmet customer needs. ODI frames customer needs as "Jobs to be Done," which offers two advantages: It helps teams focus on the efficacy of their proposed solutions, and it prevents them from getting attached to a particular idea or model. It's all about getting the job done and helping the customer.[1]

**Case Study: The Disney MagicBand**    No visitor to the Disney theme parks ever said, "You know what would make this experience even better? Wristbands that will open hotel doors, pay for souvenirs, and reserve a spot in line for my favorite ride." But leadership knew that visiting parks meant committing to waiting in lines, waiting on meals, waiting to pay for goods and services, and that Walt Disney World in particular had developed a reputation for its endless long lines.

The issue had been worsening for years with no solution in sight. Then, Meg Croften, the president of Walt Disney Parks & Resort at the time, sent her team out to better understand the "problem" so they could build the right solution. In her own words, "We were looking for pain points." A few years and nearly $1 billion later, the Disney MagicBand was born.

These wristbands contain a radio chip that transmits forty feet in every direction, communicating with systems throughout the park as wearers move about. It allows them to enter the park, check into their hotel rooms, and even make purchases without waiting or fussing with keys, wallets, or paperwork. It's the ultimate in frictionless tech.

---

[1]https://strategyn.com/outcome-driven-innovation-process/

And after MagicBands were deployed, guests began spending more money, 70 percent of first-time visitors said they planned to return (as compared to just 50 percent six years earlier), and 5,000 more people could visit the park every day since massive lines no longer clogged up pedestrian walkways. Clearly, "waiting in long lines" was the right problem for Disney to solve.[2]

# A recommended approach: Interview your customers as they speak to their experiences and perspectives related to the problem space.

**Objective:** Learn about and identify the highest impact problems to solve.

**Step 1: Talk to the people you are building for about the problem space and how they cope with or solve for it today.**

These conversations tend to be very open-ended, so we have some tips to guide you:

- **Start broad.** Don't narrow in on or ask about a specific problem right away. Stay at 30,000 feet for as long as possible. For example, if you are building for educators, ask about what they do to be effective teachers. Don't start by asking about a specific activity—like determining grades—out of the gate. If you do, you may narrow your focus prematurely.

- **Find out what works well and where there are opportunities.** Learn about the ups and downs around a particular area of their life. For example, if you're speaking with a financial advisor, they may love the relationships they build with their customers, yet struggle with the technology they use to manage their accounts. That may be a problem worth solving.

---

[2]User Friendly, pp. 216-220

- **Learn about how they are solving existing problems today.** If they are using other solutions to solve the problem—even it's a suboptimal experience—find out what they're doing, what works well, and where gaps exist. Opportunities will surface here.

## Step 2: Dig deeper into interesting areas.

As you converse with customers about the problem space and how they are solving for it today, you will stumble upon interesting areas where you'll want to learn more. Some areas that may be worthy of exploring on a deeper level include:

- **Find out if other people are involved in the decision-making process.** Who else is involved in making a critical decision? A partner or spouse? Another parent? In a B2B environment, does your end user need to convince the boss? Knowing everyone involved in the decision helps you identify and understand all the players and their needs.

- **Gather details of competitive offerings.** If a competitive offering is part of the solution today, how is it delivering? What works well? Where are the opportunities? And how might that inform the set of problems you've identified?

- **Identify any strong emotions around the problem.** Challenges with children, relationships, career evolution, and other life events are often tied to big emotions. Deeply understanding the customer's frame of mind will help you prioritize the problem or opportunity, and help you build a deep level of empathy that you can lean on as you move further down the product development process.

- **Understand the severity of problems.** This provides insight into customers' own perceptions of the problem area and can help you identify the best opportunities. Ask them to rate or prioritize different challenges you identified during your conversation.

## Step 3: Take action and socialize key learnings.

When you have conversations with customers, you'll likely be sifting through a lot of fascinating learnings. Some are immediately actionable while others may not be. If you tie back to your objective of getting to know your users so you can identify the right problem to solve, here's how you may take action on what you've collected:

- **Pair your problem list with human insight.** You likely have a list of problems you've identified from surveys or other feedback mechanisms. In addition to the number of people who have experienced each problem, capture the essence of it. What are the emotions tied to it? How severe is the problem from the customers' perspective? How much demand is there for a solution?

- **Build key learnings into your personas.** Most product teams work with a set of personas, which can be fairly flat documents containing metrics, numbers, and broad statements. Much of what you learn in these interviews can help you humanize them. Consider linking to videos clips of customer interviews from your persona documentation to bring them to life.

- **Give others a glimpse into what you've learned.** A nicely curated video of key learnings from your conversations can be shown in a team meeting or to kickoff a sprint. This can pull the team closer to the human perspective—which will power strategy and approach.

# A recommended approach: Observe your customers as they navigate the problem using existing solutions.

**Objective:** Understand the current solution, what works and what doesn't, and where there is opportunity to innovate or differentiate.

### Step 1: For those who indicate that they are solving the problem today with existing solutions, ask them to show you how.

You can find these people during broader interviews or you can specifically recruit for them. Either way, here are some tips for managing these types of user tests:

- **Jump into the solution.** Since you've already dug into the problem area and understood the pain points, you don't have to spend too much time there. Sure, revisit it briefly, but the objective here is to observe them using an existing solution.

- **Have them interact with it as they normally do.** You could ask them to start by showing you around or by giving them a scenario to walk you through, such as "Add celery to your grocery shopping list" or "Find a movie coming out next month that you could watch at a nearby theater."

- **Be prepared to skip around.** This is particularly true if you are looking at a "hacky" solution that involves two or more websites, apps, or products. For example, a family's calendar management might involve a handful of disparate calendars, a shared document, and a childcare app. This is valuable to capture, but it can be a lot to keep track of, so stay focused and organized.

### Step 2: Dig deeper into interesting areas.

As you watch them use existing solutions, you'll see and learn some interesting things that you may want to follow up on. Some areas that may be worthy of exploring on a deeper level include:

- **How they chose the solution or set of solutions.** You could start here or ask after they show you how they manage the challenge today. Regardless, it's helpful to know how they found out about, evaluated, and decided to engage with a particular solution. They might not remember or recall it correctly, but even incomplete details can be telling. This information can help you better understand what's valuable to them during their decision-making process.

- **What's most valuable.** There's a reason why they have adopted a certain approach to solving their problem. Find out what they value in the solution or set of solutions they show you.

- **Where the gaps are.** While they might have a solution today, probe on whether or not it truly meets their needs. Chances are they are using a suboptimal solution. This information will help you identify opportunities.

### Step 3: Take action and socialize key learnings.

Given we are working to identify what works well and what doesn't with an existing solution to identify opportunities, here are some likely next steps and ways to socialize your learnings:

- **Share sentiment around existing solutions.** Not only do you want to share what people are doing today to address their needs, you also want to associate the emotion or sentiment alongside it. If they're thrilled with the ways things work today, the team should know that. If they're not, the team should know that, too.

- **Sketch the existing experience.** You can do this in a document, a slide, or a prototyping tool, but the goal here is to show the experience—especially if there are multiple solutions involved—so the team can see the journey (and the likely struggles) customers are currently facing today. Again, this will help with identifying opportunities.

- **Give others a glimpse into what you've learned.** A recording of the customer using a competitive solution is bound to draw attention. This is where you want to show rather than tell.

# A recommended approach: Validate problem statements with customers.

**Objective:** Ensure you truly understand the problem before you move into the solutioning phase.

### Step 1: Ask a customer to read through a problem statement and react to it.

This is a good way to gauge whether or not you've identified a problem to solve and you understand it deeply. Some tips:

- **Keep it simple.** This doesn't have to be a thesis. Simply describe the problem you believe you'd identified, such as: "I want my home to be cozy and stylish, but I don't have the time or expertise to make changes."

- **Consider putting a few problem statements in front of them.** If you're interested in what problem statement best resonates, try putting a handful of problem statements in front of them.

### Step 2: Observe them as they review, and listen as they narrate their reactions.

As they review and react, ask yourself these questions:

- Does it seem to resonate? Do they validate it immediately or seem confused?
- Do they have a visceral reaction, such as head nodding?
- Do they add any additional details to it or try to explain it further?

### Step 3: Ask them directly about their opinions.

After you get their immediate reaction and perhaps a few comments, you probably want to dig in deeper. Some ideas:

- **Get their initial reaction.** When they first saw it, were they in agreement with the problem statement? Or did they look confused? Ask them to reflect on their first impressions.
- **Understand what is missing or doesn't make sense.** The problem statement may roughly make sense, but they might not agree with some details or they may add additional information to it. All good feedback to get.
- **Learn how it fits amongst other problems you've identified.** If you're getting feedback on more than one problem statement, ask them to prioritize and explain their reasoning around why one problem feels like a higher priority than others.

### Step 4: Share and take action on key learnings.

This is where you are gauging reactions to the problem statements to see if the team truly understands the problem before you move into solutioning. Here are some likely next steps:

- **Address big disconnects.** If the problem statement isn't something people resonate with, go back to the drawing board. It can be disappointing, but remember that solving the wrong problem is a huge waste of time and money. Better to figure it out now and pivot.

- **Tweak, tweak, tweak.** You may be close, but you will likely need to add more detail or change some of the problem description. Go ahead and do that before moving into solutioning, but make sure you validate the *updated* problem statement, too.

- **Share the validation—or pushback—with the team.** This feedback is best when it comes straight from the customer. Share some video highlights from your user test with team members who may not have been able to attend.

# Building the Right Solution

**Why is This Important?**   In order to serve customers, create stellar experiences, and stand out among your competitors, you must make sure you're bringing the right solution to market.

Most product development teams are keenly aware that the majority of new products fail; around 80 percent of the offerings that hit the market tank quickly and expensively. The reasons are manifold. Perhaps the new product couldn't oust a longtime customer favorite. Maybe the new product was aesthetically wonderful, but so hard to use that everyone gave up. Or maybe, despite being a superior product, the marketing and go-to-market efforts failed to compel target customers to buy.

As a product manager, you're balancing business priorities, customer needs, and technical challenges in the face of tight deadlines. All that pressure may cause you and your team to go charging down a certain path without thoroughly determining your approach or concept is the right one.

Although there's no way to create a fail-proof offering, validating proposed solutions and value propositions before you build anything certainly helps. By vetting multiple concepts and gathering human insight at this stage, you widen your opportunity to succeed and position yourself to avoid major product flops.

So, how do you do this? Gathering human insight at this phase forces teams to thoroughly explore multiple solutions before settling on the single, best one.

And here's the good news: You don't have to drop a single line of code to capture human insight at this stage. You can show people a sketch, a written value prop, or rough concepts. You can even show users something your competitors have already done that you're considering building and ask, "What are your thoughts on this?"

**Bottom line:**   Show your ideas to people, observe them, and gather their input before moving into true development.

No matter how well you think you know your users at this point, testing your concepts with them is still crucial. Your team will be too close to the project to be objective. Fresh eyes and perspectives from real or potential customers are essential to ensure you keep them at the center of your process.

**Case study: Notre Dame IDEA Center**   Notre Dame's IDEA Center shepherds the university community's best business ideas to the marketplace. Standing for Innovation, De-Risking, and Enterprise Acceleration, the IDEA Center works with faculty, students, communities, and alumni entrepreneurs on their commercially viable, early-stage product ideas and innovations.

But testing market viability with early stage companies can sometimes include very technical or niche concepts. Whether teams are working on spices made with vitamins, an at-home breast cancer diagnostics solution, or an apparel brand, all IDEA Center startups need to go through a rigorous market assessment.

As an idea, innovation, or startup moves forward, the team begins working with Ben Hoggan, the center's Director of De-Risking. The teams conduct a mix of interviews and user tests as they attempt to answer four questions:

1. Does the product or service idea work?
2. What is the problem they are solving?
3. Does anyone want to buy it, and who?
4. And are they going to love using it?

When teams began getting perspectives through the eyes of potential customers, the quality of solutions flowing through IDEA Center skyrocketed. The ability to learn and share what customers were saying about the business concepts, good or bad, forced teams to hone in on perfect-fit solutions instead of pushing through good-enough ideas.

By integrating customer perspectives earlier in the process, the team was able to increase reach and impact. In 2019, the IDEA Center doubled the number of companies that were started in the previous two years. Those 64 companies reported raising $6.6 million in investment and generating $10.9 million in product sales, a 584% year-over-year increase from 2018.

## Building the Solution Right

**Why Is This Important?**   This is the stage where most companies do user testing even if they've skipped it at previous stages. As we've said before, if you user test a nearly finished or ready-to-launch product and find that people don't like or want to use your solution, you have to go back to the drawing board. That's painful and expensive. All the more reason to do this work early and often. The feedback you get here should result in tweaks, not huge redesigns or resets.

Asking people to use an early design or prototype and then observing them as they do it can be one of the most powerful ways to make a direct connection with your customers, see what works and what doesn't, and walk away with tangible, actionable feedback. We often have assumptions about how our customers will use something, but without observing them as they navigate an experience, we don't really know how it's working, if it's meeting their expectations and needs, or how we can improve or optimize.

# A recommended approach: Review multiple concepts or ideas with potential customers.

**Objective:** Choose the right solution to bring to market.

**Step 1: Put two or more concepts or ideas in front of a potential customer, and ask them to react to and evaluate them.**

Once you've decided on the ideas you'd like customer perspectives on, it's as simple as putting those ideas in front of them and asking. Some tips to keep in mind:

- **You can get feedback on anything in any state.** A tiny feature, a brand new product concept, something that is sketched on a whiteboard, or something that looks more polished are all viable options to pressure test.

- **Don't weed out the ideas you don't like before getting customer perspective.** Doing so puts you at risk for narrowing in on a solution prematurely. Remember: You are not your customer.

- **Consider the order in which you show options to customers.** You may want to mix it up to avoid the potential of everyone picking option number one because it's the first one they saw.

## Step 2: Observe them as they examine the options and listen as they narrate their observations.

As they review and react, consider these questions:

- What facial expressions or body language do they offer as they look at your concepts or ideas?
- What one do they gravitate towards initially?
- If they choose a "winner," is it a clear choice? Or do they hesitate? Do they want to combine a couple concepts together instead?
- What one do they think is "best"? What one is the loser? Why?
- Is the "best" solution truly optimal? What might they change or improve?

## Step 3: Ask them directly about their opinions.

After they've reviewed and shared their feedback, it's time to dig a bit deeper. Some areas you may want to explore:

- **Find out if any concepts truly address the core problem.** Solicit input from people you're sure suffer from the problem you're addressing to see if your proposed offerings will really help them. If they won't, be prepared to pivot.
- **Determine the value each concept provides.** Ask them to explain the value of each concept or idea in their own words. You'll learn a lot about what's important to them and what problem they believe it will solve.
- **Learn why they prefer a certain concept.** Having an explanation of the option they prefer and why will provide much more context than just their selection alone.
- **Learn why they dismiss certain concepts.** This can help the team understand what to discard and what to avoid in the future.
- **Find out what they might improve about the preferred concept.** Although they may have a favorite or preference, they probably have some ideas for improvement, too. Collect that perspective.
- **Determine propensity to use the proposed concept.** This can be tricky and not always reliable, but it's usually worthwhile to explore. A rating scale question with an explanation of their rating works well here.

- **Identify the features that are most useful or important.** If you're getting feedback on larger concepts, you can start asking customers about the features they may value most. Consider asking them to group desired features by high, medium, and low priority.

### Step 4: Share & take action on key learnings.

Asking customers to compare a handful of options can help the team make a decision about a direction to take. Here's what you may do with your learnings:

- **Make a decision.** Typically, you see trends and themes pretty quickly on what concepts or ideas people prefer, and you will likely be able to march forward with a decision that the team feels confident about. This is especially true if the trends from your user tests align with some quantitative data—like a survey that captures preference.

- **Iterate.** Oftentimes, you'll identify a preferred version but with some suggested enhancements. The team will likely want to incorporate the feedback and test again before moving on.

- **Go back to the drawing board.** There's a chance that customers may not see value in any of the concepts you put in front of them. That's OK. You're catching this feedback early and can address it. Better to learn this now than launch a product that fails.

- **Share your customers' preference with others internally.** There is no shortage of opinions when it comes to product concepts, so accompanying internal stakeholder feedback with clear customer perspectives can help everyone feel confident about the direction.

**Case Study: Pediatric Health System**    One of largest pediatric health systems in the United States wanted to update its website and apps, which are hubs of critical information that help to attract prospective patients and keep current patients informed. Given the large scale of the project and the small scale of the lean team working on it, they sought to rebuild the website template by template. Using this approach, they could create optimized designs that could then be applied across all relevant webpages—for rapid change at scale as well as consistency throughout the digital experience.

Starting with the template used on department and program pages of the website, the team gathered feedback to figure out what was working, what wasn't, what people liked, and what needed to change.

Using these insights, the team created a wireframe of a potential new design. They then sought feedback on the revised wireframe as well. Once the winning template design was finalized, the team ran a pilot using the updated design on two department pages.

After one month, one department page saw a 27.2 percent increase in requests for an appointment, and another department page saw an astonishing 39.8 percent increase in appointment requests. The year-over-year increases were even more impressive: a 58.5 percent and 56.8 percent increase, respectively.

## A recommended approach: User test your early designs and prototypes

**Objective:** Ensure your product is easy to use, especially for flows and experiences that impact KPIs.

**Step 1: Ask a user to complete an activity that is central to your solution while narrating their thoughts aloud.**

It can be overwhelming to think about where and how to start, so keep these tips in mind:

- **Start broad.** Don't focus them on a specific part of the experience right away. Unless that is, in fact, the only thing you need feedback on. Instead, ask them to explore a bit before pointing them to a specific activity—like finding product details or contact information.
- **Don't help them.** This is really hard. Every ounce of you will want to show or guide them, but remember: You won't be there to do that when the other hundreds, thousands, or millions of people are using

the experience. Stay quiet so you gather unbiased feedback that will help you improve.

- **Be quiet.** Don't engage in ongoing conversation. Sure, you need to ask them to try a few things and give them some instructions, but try not to converse with them while they engage with the experience. Doing so will distract them and will make it harder for you to take everything in. Subtle acknowledgments—such as "OK" or "nodding your head" can communicate that you are there and paying attention, but anything beyond that will only distract. You'll have plenty of time to talk to them at the end of your session.

### Step 2: Observe them as they walk through the process, and listen as they narrate their observations and interactions.

There's a lot that happens at a rapid pace during a user test of a prototype. Consider these questions as you observe and listen:

- When they are given an activity to complete, do they quickly know what to do and where to start? Or do they hesitate a bit?
- Are they able to move easily through the experience?
- Where are the snags?
- Can they find and understand crucial information as they proceed?
- Can they fill out forms or fields without any trouble?
- How long does it take for them to complete each step? The full process?
- What challenges or mistakes do they encounter along the way?

### Step 3: Ask them about the experience.

After they try different activities using a prototype, you will likely have questions for them. Some to consider are:

- **What worked well.** This will help the team understand what is working well now and what to retain in future iterations.
- **What was confusing.** This will help the team identify perceived challenges and hiccups, as well as what to focus on improving in the next iteration.

- **How they felt while using it.** They may have been able to zip through various activities, but if the experience was lackluster or didn't meet their expectations, you need to know that.

- **How confident they are that they did what you asked them to do correctly.** If they are wildly confident that they did all the activities given to them, but you noticed they didn't successfully complete most, that's a disconnect that needs to be addressed.

- **What they might improve.** Although customers don't always know what they need or what improvements are necessary, it can be helpful to gather this perspective. You may get some gems just by asking.

### Step 4: Share and take action on key learnings.

You'll likely walk away with tons of notes and ideas after just a handful of people have used your early design or prototype. It's important you take action on key learnings. Try not to succumb to analysis paralysis. Here are some typical next steps after a user test:

- **Identify high-priority issues to address.** Typically, a handful of issues will arise that everyone experienced. For example, everyone was confused by the pricing or no one could find the membership details. Determine the ones that were showstoppers and/or tied to KPIs, and gather the team to address. Once you improve your approach, you should user test again.

- **Log issues that may not be addressed right away.** Not everything you observe and capture can be addressed before the next iteration or improvement. Capture these so you can look back over time to ensure they get addressed eventually. There's a good chance that many will go away over time as you pivot or shift your approach, but track them just in case.

- **Plan for your next round of feedback.** With the issues you've captured, you'll likely need to make some improvements and you should build user testing into your plan. No experience is ever perfect. Your next round of feedback may be another user test of the improved prototype or it could be a round of card sorting to address critical navigation challenges. (See sidebar for details on cardsorting.)

- **Share findings and accompanying video clips—both good and bad—with others.** What you observed, heard, and captured in your user tests should be shared. You can bring in lunch and have everyone watch the sessions together or you could get creative with the recordings and create a "highlights" and "lowlights" compilation to communicate what worked well and where the team needs to focus next.

## Card Sorting

Card sorting helps teams group, label, and describe information more effectively based on customer input. Most commonly, this tactic is used when designing (or redesigning) the navigation or content organization of a digital experience. And that's because it helps to design information architecture—or the grouping of categories of content, the hierarchy of those categories, and the labels used to describe them.

Card sorting requires you to create a set of cards—either digital or physical—to represent each concept or item. These cards will then be grouped or categorized by your users in ways that make the most sense to them. For best results, you'll need to decide if you want to run an open, closed, or hybrid card sort. The approach you choose will greatly depend on what you want to find out.

### Open card sort

In an open card sort, participants sort cards into categories that make sense to them and label each category themselves. This approach gives your users the most authority to group and categorize information how they see fit. Once they've organized the cards into groups, they will then have to name each grouping—providing maximum insight into your customers' thought processes.

If you're unsure how to design or categorize your website, an open card sort can help. It provides feedback from your users about what they find relevant and necessary to group. With these groupings, you can make your website more attuned to your user's interests and needs.

*(continued)*

*(continued)*

## Closed card sort

In a closed card sort, participants sort cards into categories you give them. This approach is useful when the labels for something are pre-scribed or have already been set. In this scenario, your users would be responsible for organizing the cards into a sitemap that already exists.

Ultimately, its purpose is to see if your existing categories seem logical. As a bonus, it's also great if you need to add a bunch of new content to a site or if existing content needs to be reorganized.

## Hybrid card sort

In a hybrid card sort, participants sort cards into categories you give them but may also create their own categories if they choose. Nor-mally, this technique is used when the team already has some cat-egories established but would like their customer's input as to what the others could be.

# The Path to Launch Should Be Fueled with Human Insight

Understanding your customers is the key to ensuring that you pro-vide them with what they want, and minimize what they find frus-trating or challenging. Whether it's a physical product or a digital experience, you're more likely to meet—and exceed—customer expectations if you integrate user testing throughout the product development process. That way, at each step, you're creating solu-tions and experiences that match what your customers are seeking.

The bottom line is: Let feedback from your customers be your guid-ing light—your proverbial North Star—to ensure that all the work, time, and other resources you put into creating product experiences line up with what your customers want.

# CHAPTER 8

# Marketing

## Getting Inside the Heads of Your Buyers

S o your colleagues in product design are launching a new product or optimizing an existing one, and you are working alongside them as you figure out what campaigns to launch, how to structure pricing, how to update or refine your messaging and your brand, how to reach your target audience, and a plethora of other activities meant to drive demand, brand awareness, sales, and ongoing loyalty.

To ensure you connect with your customers authentically and effectively, you have to talk to them, observe them, create with their preferences in mind, and cultivate ongoing empathy and understanding.

And if the old adage is true and it takes an average of seven interactions with your brand before a purchase will take place,[1] how can you ensure potential customers don't get turned off by your efforts? Customer experience isn't just about buying and using products, it's about the impressions and feelings people have when they interact with a brand or company.

---

[1]https://www.b2bmarketing.net/en/resources/blog/marketing-rule-7-and-why-its-still-relevant-b2b

In this chapter, we will cover how to gather human insight to inform your marketing messages, visuals, and strategies during three of the six key moments in the overall customer journey, including:

1. Recognizing a problem and having an interest in fixing it
2. Researching and comparing solutions
3. Choosing a company or solution to solve the problem

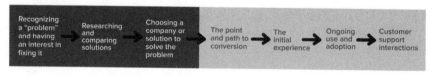

**FIGURE 8.1**   Using Human Insight to Inform Your Marketing Efforts

We recognize that this end-to-end process may happen in minutes, weeks, months, and, in some cases, years. Note that each time an individual interacts with you, it gets added to the larger overall experience they have with you and your company.

# Recognizing a "Problem" and Having an Interest in "Fixing" It

The first step that customers take in doing business or re-engaging with you is recognition or realizing that something in their life is broken and worthy of fixing. Sometimes this happens organically, and sometimes the process can be accelerated. As most marketers know, you can help people reach this step by describing pain points or needs in your messaging that reflect the experiences and resonate with the intended audience.

# Researching and Comparing Solutions

This is where your customers start to look for solutions to their problems, vet different offerings, and, in some cases, split hairs. If you're unable to present your offering or services in a way that speaks to your customers and differentiates you from all the noise, you'll lose out. This is all about your positioning and go-to-market strategy; product naming, price, how you describe the value you provide, and all the tiny details of your product or offering matter here.

# Choosing a Company or Solution to Solve the Problem

After exploring potential solutions—which may be a short or long endeavor—customers ultimately decide who they want to give their time, attention, and money to in exchange for a fix or to fulfill a need.

This choice can be driven by a motivated customer looking to find the right solution, or it can be prompted by a company that shows up at the right place at the right time when a customer's life has otherwise gotten in the way and delayed the decision.

Knowing how and where to show up—both when customers seek you out and when you push your offering to an Instagram feed or via a perfectly timed email—requires human insight.

# Human Insight for Building Awareness and Gaining Customers

When capturing customer perspectives during the three critical phases of early awareness and the "pre"-customer experience we covered previously, marketing teams typically use a many-pronged approach to pulling human insight into their key decisions. The focus of user tests they use to glean human insight covers:

- Understanding the problem and your customers
- Vetting value prop, messaging, positioning, and calls to action

- Gathering reactions to creative content and campaigns
- Comparison testing (of just about anything and everything)
- Optimizing key conversion points tied to ongoing communication

We cover the importance of each, share a case study, and offer a recommended user testing approach for you to adopt.

## Understanding the Problem and Your Customers. Intimately.

**Why Is This Important?**    Marketers play a central role in the success of modern companies. They're tasked with multiple business priorities including improving brand reputation, increasing customer loyalty, generating demand, driving revenue, and much more. And the scope of responsibilities marketers face has only expanded as organizations attempt to keep up with the ever-evolving needs of the customer.

This leaves marketers little time to dig deep into user testing and human insight, which can lead to tone-deaf campaigns, ads that fall flat, and messaging that doesn't speak to potential customers. We can't emphasize this enough: Marketers who perform user tests to deeply understand customer needs, pain points, and perspectives have a much better chance of creating messaging and positioning that resonates, promoting the messages and offers using channels that your customers use, and doing it in a compelling way that quickly converts prospects into customers.

**Case Study: Thomas Cook Group**    The Thomas Cook Group has been a household name in Europe for nearly 200 years, trusted across the continent for arranging and booking holiday travel. When the company was forced to liquidate in September 2019, it sent shockwaves through the entire travel industry and many people assumed it would never return.

Within weeks, a small group of spirited former colleagues had developed a business plan, secured investment from a major Chinese leisure groups, and set to work building a new digital-only Thomas Cook that was worthy of the original name. COVID-19 swept across the world as this plan was being enacted, but a determined leadership knew that Thomas Cook would be a trusted name once the damage caused by COVID-19 had eased. And by September of 2020, the new Thomas Cook website was live and open to customers both new and old.

Jo Migom, chief digital and marketing officer for Thomas Cook, says that human insight was instrumental to the relaunch. Even shortly after the liquidation, she and her team quickly discovered that customer sentiment was overwhelmingly positive. The nostalgia and emotional connections people had with the brand were strong and pervasive, since so many had fond memories of envisioning and booking wonderful vacations with Thomas Cook.

"We kept monitoring customer sentiment which was imperative because the brand had been affected," she explains. "That is something we absolutely acknowledged. But when speaking to customers about it, we could feel that there was such passion for this brand as well as great sadness that it was no longer. That was a key driver for us to keep our motivation high as we began to bring it back."

Once the frameworks were in place, Migom and her team ran user tests on the website without telling people it was Thomas Cook. When people were finally told they were reviewing the proposed new site for the travel company, they were overjoyed to learn they'd be able to plan vacations through this trusted brand again. In fact, the team shared these reactions with executives, and those authentic, emotional reactions helped them gain a higher level of support for launching the digital experience. As Jo describes the power of having executives see customer emotions firsthand, she says, "It's about winning hearts and minds, not just minds."

Now Thomas Cook is a fully digital brand and continues to gather customer input from multiple places to create a holistic view of the customer. Through big data and human insight, the company continually tracks customer needs and incorporates their suggestions. Thomas Cook measures customer satisfaction before booking, after booking, and after travel, and that information is incorporated into every team member's objectives. This effort to understand customers continually and intimately is paying off: Migom reports that customer satisfaction ratings are four times those of the old business and the website now ranks among the best of its peers on Trustpilot.

# A recommended approach: Interview your customers about the problem space and existing solutions.

**Objective:** Get to know your potential customers so you can speak their language, position your offerings against their true needs, and build authentic connections.

**Step 1: Talk to your target customers and listen to how they speak to the problem and their needs.**

These conversations tend to be very open-ended, so we have some tips to guide you:

- **Start broad.** Don't narrow in on or ask about a specific problem right away. Stay at 30,000 feet for as long as possible. For example, if you are creating for car buyers, ask about what they do when they are considering a new car purchase. Don't start by asking about a specific activity—like car financing—out of the gate. If you do, you may not capture how they speak about their core needs and the problem area, which means you will lose key context that should inform your positioning and go-to-market strategy.
- **Find out what works well and where there are opportunities.** Learn about the ups and downs around a particular area of their lives.

For example, if you're speaking with a busy parent, they may want to make more family memories, yet struggle with meal planning and cooking—which takes away from family time. That may be something you can lean into when developing your messaging and positioning

- **Learn about how they are solving existing problems today.** If they are using other solutions to solve the problem—even it's a suboptimal experience—find out what works well and where the gaps are. This will help with messaging to differentiate and stand out from the noise.

### Step 2: Dig deeper into interesting areas.

As you converse with customers about the problem space and how they are solving for it today, you will stumble upon interesting areas where you'll want to learn more. Some areas that may be worthy of exploring on a deeper level include:

- **Other people involved in the decision-making process.** Who else is involved in making a critical decision? A partner or spouse? Another parent? In a B2B environment, does your end user need to convince the boss? Knowing everyone involved in the decision or ecosystem helps you identify and understand all the players and their needs—and how to best message to each.

- **Details of competitive offerings.** If a competitive offering is part of the solution today, how is it delivering? What works well? Where are the opportunities? And how can you build that into your marketing strategy?

- **Strong emotions around the problem.** Challenges with children, relationships, career evolution, and other life events are often tied to big emotions. Deeply understanding the customer's frame of mind will help you build empathic and authentic messaging and positioning.

- **The severity of problem areas.** This provides insight into customers' own perceptions of the problem area, and can help you identify the best opportunities. Ask them to rate or prioritize different challenges you identified during your conversation.

### Step 3: Take action and socialize key learnings.

When you have conversations and interviews with potential customers, you'll likely be sifting through a lot of insights. Some are immediately actionable while others may not be. If we tie back to our objective of getting to know your potential customers so you can speak their language, position your offerings against their true needs, and build authentic connections, you may do the following with what you've collected.

- **Add another dimension to your personas, customer segmentations, or ICPs.** Remember that your customers are people, not segmentation models or ICPs. Empathy maps (see sidebar in this chapter) are a good way to humanize personas and other customer profile documentation.

- **Capture themes you heard around the problem space, what they need, and the emotions that are tied to it.** Use these themes to influence messaging, positioning, and other marketing-related content.

- **Give others a glimpse into what you've learned.** A nicely curated video of key learnings from your conversations can be shown in a team meeting or to kickoff a new campaign. This can pull the team closer to the human perspective—which can power strategy and approach.

## Empathy Maps

An empathy map is a collaborative tool that teams can use to learn more about their customers. Much like personas, empathy maps often represent a group of users, such as a customer segment. Since these maps externalize knowledge about users, they help teams to create a shared understanding for decision-making.

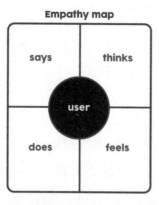

**FIGURE 8.2** Empathy Map

To create an empathy map, ask your team to bring any human insight about the customer or segment you want to build a stronger shared understanding around. Sketch the empathy map template on a large piece of paper or (digital) whiteboard at the front of the room. Give each team member a set of (digital) sticky notes and a marker, then ask them to write each individual piece of information they possess about the customer on a separate note. Ideally, this understanding has been built through user testing.

Each team member should place their notes on the map while explaining their logic, and can pause to ask or answer questions from other members of the group. The discussion that is generated will help bring the customer to life and surface deeper insights about their needs, thoughts, and feelings.

The empathy map should be a referenceable resource to help everyone better understand customers as humans—not data points.

# A recommended approach: Understanding how people think about the problem by observing them "search" for a solution.

**Objective:** Inform your content and marketing strategies to be more effective, including your SEO and paid search listing approaches.

**Step 1: Ask a potential customer to pull up the search engine of their choice, tee up the "problem" you'd like them to solve, and have them find a potential solution.**

Understanding how your potential customer uses a search engine to locate a solution will help you pinpoint the right language to use across the board. Some tips to keep in mind while you do so:

- **As you tee up the problem, keep your language as general as possible.** Try not to use language that may influence how they search or the terms they use.

- **Ask them to use whatever search engine they prefer.** This will be most comfortable for them and you will get the most authentic insights.

**Step 2: Observe them as they formulate their search terms, and listen as they narrate their observations and interactions with the results they get back.**

Consider these questions as you watch:

- Do they start typing immediately or do they sit and ponder before starting to search?
- Do they type in words that are different from the ones they say aloud?
- Do they express any confusion or frustration deciding what terms to use?
- Are the results relevant? Do they find what they need right away?
- What results do they engage with, and in what order?
- What competitive offerings do they engage with, and why?
- Where are the opportunities for you to show up or differentiate?

**Step 3: Ask them about their experience and opinions.**

This is your chance to dig deeper on interesting moments. Some areas that may be worth exploring a bit deeper include:

- **Words they used to formulate their search.** Even simple questions like, "I see you used the word 'budget app' while searching for solutions to managing your money. Can you say more about why you chose that particular approach?" will likely get them to expand on their motivations and thought process.

- **Interactions with search results.** Why did they click certain listings? What was compelling? Why did they skip others?

- **Satisfaction with results.** Did they find what they needed? How hard was it to get to something relevant? And did this match their expectations?

### Step 5: Share and take action on key learnings.

As always, do something with what you've captured and learned. Some actions you may take include:

- **Use search terms, queries, and competitive intel to inform your marketing and go-to-market strategy**. Everything from product naming to value prop and pricing can be influenced by the search queries people use around the problem space.

- **Iterate on your SEO strategy to include the words and phrases that your potential customers are using.** Integrating keywords into certain elements of your experience, such as headings and page titles, can help you show up at the top of search results.

- **Compare common search terms and queries against the words or phrases you bid on in your paid search strategy and adjust as needed.** This will allow you to invest in keywords that will likely give you a return.

- **Socialize your learnings.** Imagine watching ten potential customers search for something your company supports in rapid succession. In addition to looking at reports from analytics, this will add a rich dimension to the team's understanding of what potential customers truly need. The insights you collect from watching people search for solutions to a problem should be shared with teams that make decisions on the content strategy, messaging and positioning, go-to-market strategy, and the SEO and paid search strategies.

# Vetting the Value Prop, Messaging, Positioning, and Calls to Action

**Why Is This Important?** Taglines, advertising copy, scripts, and just about any verbiage you plan to use to describe your company or offering will influence whether or not people can find you in a noisy marketplace and see immediate value. How you express your mission, describe your offerings, and speak about your company absolutely must line up with how people outside the company think and talk about those things. Otherwise, you won't reach them or win them over.

Few marketing teams have the time or money to get feedback on every piece of copy, so they often just hope their messages will resonate with customers. Instead of taking shots in the dark, we recommend user testing high-level messaging and positioning before creating any deliverables. This allows you to capture compelling customer reactions, which you can share within your organization to explain decisions, educate people, and settle disputes.

Word choice is especially critical if your company has a global footprint or if you're hoping to enter new markets in different locales. A word or phrase that has one meaning in Dallas may mean something entirely different in Prague. Even within your own country and culture, you may find that some colloquialisms or single words vary in meaning. Vocabulary is cultural, and most places are a hodgepodge of cultures, so user testing your copy and headlines before releasing them will help you nip miscommunication in the bud.

**Case Study: Media and Entertainment Company**   A US-based media & entertainment company was introducing a new feature, and the internal teams weren't sure what to name it. Some teams wanted the name to be aligned to the brand, and others wanted it to be a more recognizable term. To understand what would work best for customers, the team put the two options in front of their subscribers for their reactions.

The team learned that the branded term was considered "cute," but people didn't immediately understand what it meant or why it was relevant to them. However, the more recognizable term was quickly and easily understood by subscribers. The team moved forward with the more recognizable term as the new feature name. Human insight not only solved an internal debate, but it also led to a better customer experience.

# A recommended approach: Gather reactions to your value prop, messaging, positioning, and other content or copy.

**Objective:** Make sure your copy and content attracts, resonates, and leads to engagement.

### Step 1: Ask a potential customer to read aloud and evaluate a component of your content or copy.

Content, copy, and messaging is pervasive. It's part of everything you do. Here are some ideas on what to capture the customer perspective on:

- **Tagline or slogan.** If you are looking for input on words only, consider presenting customers with written text that hasn't been formatted or designed in any way. Get their feedback without any other branded context that may distract.
- **Product or offering names.** If you are renaming, rebranding, or starting from scratch, put product and offering names in front of potential customers before releasing them publicly.
- **Product or offering descriptions.** Often overlooked, small details about your service or product description can make or break a sale or engagement. Get these in front of potential customers to address any gaps or questions.
- **Calls to action.** Find out whether the language you've chosen feels compelling, overbearing, dull, or something else that the customer articulates on their own.
- **Email.** From the sender information and subject line to the email copy and calls to action, there are so many content-related components in email messages that can benefit from customer input.
- **Social media.** No post is too short or concise for customer feedback, especially if it could be potentially controversial or polarizing.[2]

[2]https://www.creativebloq.com/news/burger-king-iwd-tweet

## Step 2: Observe them as they review and listen as they narrate their reactions.

As they review and react, ask yourself these questions:

- Does it "click"? Do they quickly understand the value prop or messaging?
- Does it resonate? Do they attribute it to anything meaningful or valuable?
- Do they point out anything that they particularly like or dislike?
- Do they stumble over any words?
- Do they express any confusion over vocabulary, implied meanings, or concepts conveyed by the copy?

## Step 3: Ask them directly about their opinions.

They may have shared something interesting that you want to explore or you may have some general questions to get a richer perspective. Some areas you may want to explore include:

- **Their initial reaction.** When they first saw it, did they smile? Did they look confused? Ask them to reflect on their first impressions.
- **A description of the message or content in their own words.** There is no better way to gauge understanding and clarity than to ask someone to explain a concept or idea in their own words. Do it here.
- **What grabbed their attention.** What stood out to them—even if not right away? This will help you understand where people are being pulled to in your content.
- **What is missing or doesn't make sense.** It's wise to assume that you can always improve. Ask for feedback on anything that is confusing or missing from your messages.

## Step 4: Share and take action on key learnings.

There is no shortage of reworking, tweaking, iterating, and optimizing that can take place after you've gathered feedback on messaging, a value prop, and other content-related components. Here's a list of some actions you may take around input on a tagline, product name, description, call to action, email campaign, or other content component.

- **Address big disconnects.** Lots of feedback on copy can lead to incremental changes, but in some cases, it requires a reset. Look for places in your messaging where people struggled to make a connection or build a basic understanding, and consider a restart.
- **Tweak, tweak, tweak.** The wrong phrase or call to action can push business away. You should always be iterating and tweaking content and messaging as you gather ongoing customer perspectives.
- **Incorporate feedback into content and message strategy.** Teams often have documented best practices around word choice, tone of voice, and style related to content and copy. After collecting feedback, you may choose to make updates to these guidelines.
- **Share with others to inform future strategy.** You will learn more about how to improve your approach as you continue to refine and gather ongoing feedback. Don't forget to share these perspectives with others who can learn from them.

## Gather Reactions to Creative Content and Campaigns (Packaging, Ads, etc.)

**Why Is This Important?**   Launching compelling creative content and campaigns that build excitement and demand is a part of the job of a marketing team. This can take the form of landing pages, print ads, billboards, audio commercials, TV and OTT commercials, social media and email campaigns, and more. Gathering human insight will help you vet your ads and campaigns to ensure they will captivate instead of confuse or alienate potential buyers.

To give you a sense of the potential impact of poor creative content in the form of package design, consider this: Tropicana invested $35 million to change the packaging of their orange juice back in 2009. Within two months of releasing the new packaging, their sales dropped by 20 percent and they lost significant market share. The failed package redesign cost them over $50 million. Imagine if they could have vetted this design with customers before launch? Perhaps they would have avoided this costly misstep.[3]

It can be challenging to receive honest feedback on a campaign you've crafted over many months and realize you need to make substantial changes, but listening to your customers pays off. They know how they want to be spoken to, they know what resonates and what irritates, and quite often they provide perspective that will make your ads and billboards appeal to thousands of people just like them.

**Case Study: UserTesting**   We do this ourselves inside of UserTesting. We had designed a series of commercials around the concept of unexpected ways that consumers use the products they buy, and it included a scene showing someone using a Bluetooth speaker in the shower. Nothing shocking was shown, but we still wondered if the implication of nudity might concern viewers. So we gathered feedback to ensure we had a relevant concept that resonated and communicated our message, while also delighting our target audience and elevating our brand appeal.

Human insight gleaned from user testing helped inform everything from concepts to scripts. And since the feedback came quickly in the form of videos of people watching the ad and reacting to it, we could give thoughtful direction to our ad agency in a timely manner. Incorporating feedback into these new commercials led to increased confidence, 10,000 new site visitors over five months, and a sixtimes higher conversion rate for clicks to our site (0.31 percent vs avg 0.05 percent.)

---

[3]https://www.businessinsider.com/tropicana-packaging-change-failure-2013-9

# A recommended approach: Get authentic reactions to creative content and campaigns.

**Objective:** Make sure your creative content and campaigns attract, resonate, and lead to engagement.

**Step 1: Ask a potential customer to consume and evaluate your creative content or campaign.**

Below are some ideas on what to capture the customer perspective on:

- **Landing page.** Show them a mockup or a live page to gather feedback and reactions.
- **Print ad.** Even a rough version is fine for gathering gut reactions.
- **Logo.** Logos can be powerful; test yours to make sure it resonates.
- **Video content.** Whether it is an ad for online use or television, get initial reactions before airing it publicly.
- **Brand visuals.** This can be anything from a series of possible logos to fonts, web design, print or digital ads, or color schemes.
- **Campaign approach.** Show users mockups of the campaign across devices and channels (social, email, etc.) to gauge reactions.
- **Mood boards.** Get customer feedback on early concepts of look and feel to help guide decisions around what creative direction to pursue.

**Step 2: Observe them as they examine the item, image, or clip, and listen as they narrate their observations.**

As they review and react, consider these questions:

- What is their initial reaction?
- Does it resonate? Do they attribute it to anything meaningful or valuable?
- Do they point out anything that they particularly like or dislike?
- Do they express any confusion over what they're seeing?

### Step 3: Ask them directly about their opinions.

They may have shared something interesting that you want to explore or you may have some general questions to get a richer perspective. Some questions you might ask include:

- **Their initial reaction.** When they first saw it, did they smile? Did they look confused? Ask them to reflect on their first impressions.

- **A description of the creative component in their own words.** There is no better way to gauge understanding and clarity than to ask someone to explain a creative or campaign in their own words. Do it here.

- **What grabbed their attention.** What stood out to them—even if not right away? This will help you understand where people are being pulled into your creative content or campaign.

- **What is missing or doesn't make sense.** It's wise to assume that you can always improve. Ask for feedback on anything that is confusing or potentially missing from the design.

- **How the creative content makes them feel.** This is one of our favorites. Ask them to list three words that describe how the creative content or campaign makes them feel.

### Step 4: Share and take action on key learnings.

There is no shortage of reworking, tweaking, iterating, and optimizing that can take place after collecting feedback on visual or creative components. Here's a list of some actions you may take after getting feedback on a logo, landing page, billboard, or new campaign.

- **Address big disconnects.** Lots of feedback on design and visuals can lead to incremental changes, but in some cases, it requires a reset. Look for places in your approach where people struggled to make a connection or build a basic understanding, and consider a restart.

- **Tweak, tweak, tweak.** The wrong image or creative approach can push business away. You should always be iterating and tweaking your visual and design strategy as you gather ongoing customer perspectives.

- **Incorporate feedback into visual design strategy.** Teams often have documented best practices around the design, imagery, font type, logos, and graphics related to brand visuals. After collecting feedback, you may choose to make tweaks to these guidelines.

- **Share with others to inform future strategy.** You will learn more about how to improve your approach as you continue to refine and gather ongoing feedback. Don't forget to share these perspectives with others who can learn from them.

## Comparison Testing—of Just About Anything and Everything—Either Your Own Options or Your Competitors'

**Why Is This Important?**   You'll always have creative and innovative people inside the company walls contributing a steady stream of ideas, but if you don't ask for outside input, your offerings may not be optimal. Pull in the customer perspective when you are vetting a few ideas or concepts to make sure you go down the right path.

Additionally, comparing your own offerings to your competitors' offerings allows you to see where you diverge, where you beat them out, and where they outperform you. And simply user testing your competitors' products, services, websites, ads, and other parts of their business to gauge customer opinions can give you a sense of your place in the market and ideas around where you can improve.

The learnings you get from comparing potential solutions and exploring competitive offerings is priceless both for improving existing offerings and going to market with the best and highest performing new option.

**Case Study: CaringBridge**   CaringBridge, a global, nonprofit social network dedicated to helping family and friends communicate with and support loved ones during a health journey, wanted to launch a major ad campaign. In order to ensure the campaign resonated with people, CaringBridge user tested multiple options and iterations of the campaign approach and messaging, gathering feedback that helped further refine the positioning.

Since CaringBridge was able to pre-screen a variety of ad iterations before the official release, CaringBridge was confident that the final product would resonate with users. The ability to test ads for emotional impact and iterate messaging before the final ads were released contributed to a strong campaign.

# A recommended approach: Review multiple concepts with potential customers.

**Objective:** Go to market with the approach that resonates and will perform best.

**Step 1: Put two or more concepts, designs, value prop statements, etc. in front of a potential customer and ask them to react to and evaluate them.**

Once you've decided what you'd like feedback on, it's as simple as sharing the options with a customer and asking for their perspective. Some tips to keep in mind:

- **You can get feedback on anything in any state.** A couple of mock-ups, a few rough storyboards, even a handful of sketches on pieces of paper can glean meaningful insight.
- **Don't weed out the ideas you don't like before getting customer perspective.** Doing so puts you at risk for narrowing in prematurely. Remember: You are not your customer.
- **Consider the order in which you show options to customers.** You may want to mix it up to avoid the potential of everyone picking option number one because it's the first one they saw.

**Step 2: Observe them as they examine the assets and listen as they narrate their observations.**

As they review and react, consider these questions:

- What facial expressions or body language do they offer as they look at your concepts or ideas?
- What one do they gravitate towards initially?
- If they choose a "winner," is it a clear choice? Or do they hesitate? Do they want to combine a couple concepts together instead?
- What one do they think is "best"? What one is the loser? Why?
- Is the "best" solution truly optimal? What might they change or improve?

**Step 3: Ask them directly about their opinions.**

After they've reviewed and shared their feedback, it's time to dig in a bit deeper. Some areas you may want to explore include:

- **Find out if any concepts truly speak to them.** You may be positioning the right solution but doing so in a way that doesn't resonate.
- **Determine the message each idea communicates.** Ask them to explain the message or creative content in their own words. You'll learn a lot about how they perceive and interpret what you've created.
- **Learn why they prefer a certain concept or visual.** Having an explanation of What one they prefer and why will provide much more context than just their selection alone.
- **Learn why they dismiss certain concepts or creatives.** This can help the team understand what to discard and what to avoid in the future.
- **Find out what they might improve about the preferred concept.** Although they may have a favorite or preference, they probably have some ideas for improvement, too. Collect that perspective.
- **Determine likelihood to engage—and why.** This can be tricky and not always reliable, but it's usually worthwhile to explore if the concept or creative would compel them to act. A rating scale question with provided commentary of their rating works well here.

**Step 4: Share and take action on key learnings.**

Asking customers to compare a handful of options can help the team make a decision about a direction to take. Here's what you may do with your learnings.

- **Make a decision.** Typically, you see trends and themes pretty quickly on what concept or ideas people prefer, and you will likely be able to march forward with a decision that the team feels confident about. This is especially true if the trends from your user tests align with some quantitative data—like a survey that captures preference.

- **Iterate.** Oftentimes, you'll identify a preferred concept or creative but with some suggested enhancements. The team will likely want to incorporate the feedback and user test again before moving on.

- **Go back to the drawing board.** There's a chance that no concept or creative evokes the response you want. That's OK. You're catching this feedback early, and you can address it. Better to learn this now than launch a campaign that fails.

- **Share your customers' preferences with others internally.** There is no shortage of opinions when it comes to creative concepts, so accompanying internal stakeholder feedback with clear customer perspectives can help everyone feel confident about the direction.

# A recommended approach: Compare competitive positioning or creative content against yours.

**Objective:** Find ways to differentiate your messaging, positioning, and brand from the competition.

**Step 1: Put a competitive campaign, positioning, value prop statement, etc. in front of a potential customer and ask them to react to and evaluate it. Then do the same with a similar asset from your company.**

Once you've decided what you'd like feedback on, it's as simple as asking a customer to review it and share their perspective. Some tips to keep in mind:

- **You can get feedback on anything that is public facing.** Link to your competitor's homepage, landing page, app description, or an image of a billboard. Anything public is fair game to user test.

- **Consider the order in which you show options to customers.** You may want to mix it up to avoid the potential of everyone picking option number one because it's the first one they saw.

**Step 2: Observe them as they examine the assets and listen as they narrate their observations.**

As they review and react, consider these questions:

- What facial expressions or body language do they offer as they look at your competitor's asset? What about when they look at yours?

- What comparisons do they make between them? What do they initially gravitate towards?

- Do they have a clear preference? Do they hesitate? Or do they want to combine the best of both?

- Is the "best" asset truly optimal? What might they change?

**Step 3: Ask them directly about their opinions.**

After they've reviewed and shared their feedback, you'll likely have more questions. Here are some areas to explore:

- **What asset they prefer and why.** Capturing an explanation of what asset they prefer and why will provide much more context than just their selection alone.

- **Perceptions on the companies or offerings.** Surprisingly, people make a lot of assumptions based on an initial—and sometimes small— exposure to a company or offering. Ask them to offer up their thoughts and how they compare the two.

- **What they might improve.** Although they may have a favorite or preference, they probably have some ideas for improvement, too. Collect that perspective.

### Step 4: Share and take action on key learnings.

Competitive tests are often done to gain intelligence and inform your differentiation strategy. Some actions that may result in evaluating your competitor's positioning against your own include:

- **Increase or decrease marketing focus on a particular product, offering, or feature.** You will likely learn that there are some key differentiators between you and your competition, and you can ramp up or down marketing efforts related to those differences accordingly.

- **Further differentiation efforts.** You may learn some key differences in how potential customers perceive you versus your competition. In some cases, you'll find opportunities to lean into the positive differentiators and downplay the negative.

- **Share with other teams, especially the product team.** Although you have collected feedback on marketing concepts, the resulting human insights will likely be relevant or helpful for the product team who is thinking about product vision and roadmaps.

## Optimizing Key Conversion Points Tied to Ongoing Communication

**Why Is This Important?**   Here's a marketer's worst nightmare: You've gotten a user to the point where they're interested enough in your company to offer up their contact information. They're on the brink of signing up to get emails or committing to hearing from you regularly, but they can't muddle their way through the registration process. Or the sign-up form kicks them out on the second page. One confusing set of directions or glitchy interface, and your chance to capture them vanishes.

This is an aspect of marketing that has nothing to do with messaging or positioning, but still contributes to your overall success. It's a part of the customer journey where ease and comprehension rule all. No money is changing hands at these key conversion points, but if the user can't join your email list quickly and easily or download that whitepaper in an instant, they never will. You've got their attention, but these people are still deciding if they want to do business with you. Remove the friction points so they'll get to "yes" quicker.

Many marketers run A/B tests, but the problems we're discussing in this section should be fixed before these optimization tests begin. We're looking at glaring errors and deal-breaking issues that turn warm prospects cold in a few frustrating clicks.

## Case Study: T. Rowe Price

We worked with investment management firm T. Rowe Price on a thorny question about site visitors. They'd redesigned their online application process to be more streamlined, but after launch they saw that 37 percent of people who initiated the process of opening an account dropped off on the very first page.

The team was baffled since they'd done loads of prototype testing to make sure that first page was clean and hiccup-free. They knew that when it comes to forms, people balk at being asked for any information that seems arbitrary, so they slimmed down the initial input to five form fields. That's about as slim as it gets. So why would applicants abandon the process?

Based on the high abandonment rate, the T. Rowe Price team assumed the page was still too complex and daunting, and that they'd have to simplify it even more. But when T. Rowe Price gathered input from actual people, the team discovered it wasn't a simplicity issue at all. Just the opposite, in fact. People wanted to see more information about the account and product before they felt comfortable offering any information about themselves. So the firm added descriptive detail and saw the dropoff rate shrink significantly.

# A recommended approach: Observe people as they interact with key conversion points tied to building awareness and demand.

**Objective:** Improve KPIs tied to building brand awareness and demand.

**Step 1: Ask a user to interact with an experience that results in follow-up from the company, such as an email signup process or a contact form.**

There are plenty of conversion points tied to awareness and demand that you can pulse to ensure they are meeting expectations and not tripping people up. The more seamless the experience, the more potential customers you can capture.

- **Forms on landing pages, white paper downloads, etc.** Forms are a common way to capture prospect details so you can keep them updated on new offerings, promotions, and campaigns. Make sure they're easy to fill out and don't ask for unnecessary details.

- **Email registration.** This flow seems simple, but if you have a double opt-in process or are asking for too much information, you may lose people along the way. User test it to make sure it's seamless.

- **Text signups.** Capturing mobile numbers to send promotions or updates via text is a newer channel that both businesses and customers have adopted. Make sure the sign up process is smooth by user testing it.

**Step 2: Observe them as they walk through the process, and listen as they narrate their observations and interactions.**

These tests tend to be fairly quick and straightforward, but you'll want to ask yourself some questions as you observe people using these experiences.

- When they are given an activity to complete, do they quickly know what to do and where to start? Or do they hesitate a bit?
- Can they fill out forms or fields without any trouble?
- Do they understand what they are signing up for?
- Are you asking for any unnecessary details?
- How long does it take for them to sign up or register?
- What challenges or mistakes do they encounter along the way?

**Step 3: Ask them about the experience.**

After they sign up, register, or subscribe, you will likely have questions for them. Some to consider are:

- **What worked well and what was confusing.** It's a rather short, simplistic experience, but there are likely some things that stood out to customers as good or bad. Ask them about their perspectives.
- **How confident they are that they did what you asked them to do correctly.** Some signup processes, such as email subscription sign-ups, require customers to confirm the subscription by clicking a button in a confirmation email. If you're testing this flow and the customer did not confirm the subscription but believes they've signed up, you've got a problem. Make sure you ask about how certain they are that they did in fact sign up, register, or subscribe.
- **What they expect to happen next.** Now that they've signed up, registered, or subscribed, what do they think will happen next? What type of information do they expect to receive? And does that match reality?

**Step 4: Share and take action on key learnings.**

While these sessions are fairly straightforward and focused, you'll likely walk away with some very actionable next steps.

- **Identify and address conversion blockers.** Anything that prevents people from successfully registering or signing up should be addressed. Issues such as streamlining forms and making the double authentication process clearer are two common findings that come out of this user testing approach.

- **Make changes and test again.** If you make adjustments to the experience based on a user test, make sure you test it again to ensure it's foolproof. These interactions tend to be small in scope but have a big impact if they don't work as expected.

- **Share findings and accompanying video clips, especially for the blockers that require convincing to fix.** If you've uncovered issues that will require some convincing to change (for example, removing a field on a form), compile a video showing a handful of people running into the same hiccup. People can't argue when they see the evidence first hand.

# The Customer Journey Continues ...

Convincing thousands of people that you've got the right solution for them is the essential first step in landing their business. But there's much more that companies need to do—and user test—to get and keep those folks as loyal customers.

# CHAPTER 9

# Every Team Owns the Experience

## Optimizing the Holistic Customer Journey

An experience begins before someone becomes a customer and builds over time across the holistic customer journey. And so while many experiences within the overall customer journey happen in isolation, it's important to remember that they all add up to one overarching experience customers have with you.

Delightful experiences cement loyalty, but that loyalty can be yanked as soon as a terrible experience arises. For this reason, it's incredibly important to continue to hone and refine the experience you provide once people decide to convert, purchase, sign up, or otherwise indicate that they want to do business with you.

Consider something like air travel. The experience of a single traveler is impacted by a variety of activities owned by dozens of different working groups. She may use the app to book or rebook, a kiosk to check in, and chat with a customer service rep at the gate. She may get emails or text messages updating her on her flight or need to use a chat function on the website to confirm a detail of her itinerary. Then there's the in-flight experience, including printed materials and instructional safety videos. You get the picture. The team who works on text messaging is unlikely to work closely with the team who edits the in-flight magazine, but both of them contribute to the overall experience.

Ongoing customer engagement and the creation of delightful experiences doesn't live in a single department, team, or division, and that means it can be challenging to manage and continually optimize.

Research shows that 75 percent of companies think they're customer-centric, yet only 30 percent of their customers agree. Informing and optimizing the overall customer journey with human insight will put you among the elite organizations that truly *do* put their customers first.

In this chapter, we will cover how to gather human insight around the remaining three of six key moments in the overall customer journey, including:

1. The point and path to conversion

2. The initial experience

3. Ongoing use and adoption

4. Customer support interactions

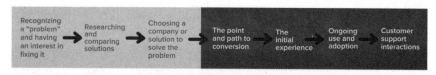

**FIGURE 9.1**   Using Human Insight Across the Holistic Customer Journey

And, since these interactions don't happen in isolation, we'll also cover how to capture the holistic experience you provide over time and across multiple touchpoints throughout the customer lifecycle.

## The Path to and Point of Conversion

Many companies get a little obsessive about their shopping carts, signup forms, checkout processes, and app download experiences. Since this is the exact spot in the customer journey where commitment takes place or money changes hands, this obsession is understandable.

It's critical that your customers can move from prospect to customer quickly and easily or they'll look elsewhere to fulfill their needs. However, a great conversion process will *never* be the one thing that cements loyalty in your buyers. Optimize the cart experience, streamline signups, and make sure conversions can happen without a hitch, but don't assume streamlining these steps is all that matters.

## The Initial Experience

Buying or signing up for stuff isn't the end of the line for all users. In many cases, it's the beginning of a long-term relationship between a customer and an organization. The first time a customer downloads and uses your app, lands on your website by clicking on a search result, or sets up an account through your health insurance portal will greatly influence their opinion of your organization. This is especially true for B2B models since most of them are tied to successful onboarding and continued use.

Gathering feedback on initial customer experiences is especially important for emerging industries and business models, because their offerings will be exponentially more unfamiliar to potentially loyal customers. If you're helping finance novices learn about and invest in cryptocurrency through an app, you need to ensure that their initial interactions are straightforward and clear. Even more than businesses in established niches, you need to ensure those very first interactions are easy, successful, and rewarding. And don't forget about physical products, too. Unboxing a new pair of shoes, a new mobile device, or a new digital thermostat all have potential to be great and memorable experiences.

## Ongoing Use and Adoption

Most companies know that customer engagement doesn't stop after that first experience, but surprisingly few of them make improvements to the longer term customer journey. So, as you might imagine, the ones that monitor for months or even years after an initial experience or onboarding gain a distinct advantage over their competitors.

Refining the interactions that make top-notch customer experiences should be as much a part of your business as setting budgets and scheduling launches.

## Customer Support Interaction

The final component of a customer journey is the help desk, customer support mechanisms, or any other functions that involve troubleshooting. If they're enthusiastically engaged up to the point they need to seek help, then thwarted or confused, that can be disastrous.

# Human Insight for the Holistic Customer Journey

When evaluating the entire customer journey or narrowing in on one of the specific touchpoints listed previously, teams typically gather human insight in four main ways, including:

- Regular health checkups on the existing experience
- Data-driven investigations
- Competitive assessments
- Customer journey tracking

We cover the importance of each, share a case study, and offer a recommended approach in the following section.

## Regular Health Checkups on Existing Experiences

**Why Is This Important?**   Let's face it. Most teams are launching new features, adding to the code base, and pushing out design updates on a near-constant basis. For this reason, it's important that you have a regular way of assessing the experience of critical touch points over time.

Regular assessments of existing experiences comprise a proactive approach that the best and brightest embrace. Instead of waiting for problems to arise and reacting to them, you can get ahead of the mess, headache, and dings on your brand or business by being proactive. Even if nothing is obviously wrong, a quarterly or bi-annual check will help you find out where the customer experience can be improved.

To make the most of regular testing, be sure to create a standardized approach that can be repeated at regular intervals. This will enable you to keep a running record of results and track improvement (or decline) over time. You might ask users to walk through the process of setting up a new bank account, finding and downloading an app, or registering for a service. Or you might create your own set of processes to vet this series of actions. Whatever you do, codify and repeat.

**Case Study: Krikey**   Krikey is a provider of mobile augmented reality (AR) games designed for an audience in India. The company was curious to run a health check of their Google Play Store page to see if any changes or optimizations could be made. Users provided very strong feedback on what language to use and how to rewrite Krikey's product description. The company didn't expect such candid input, but took it all to heart since they wanted to be sure their app fit into the market standard and aligned with user expectations.

Users also had strong opinions about Krikey's Google Play Store images. Initially the page included vertical images showcasing full-screen visuals of the games, and users could scroll through these to get a sense of what using this app might be like. Nearly every user commented that because Krikey was an AR app, they wanted to see AR in the images. The company had AR shots in the images, so this feedback stymied them at first. They wisely ran another round of tests, and in an interview one user explained that he wanted to see the game characters "coming out" of the phone.

Krikey quickly edited an image with the main game character stepping out of the phone frame and aiming a bow and arrow at a monster. This change made a huge difference in people's understanding of the app on the Google Play Store page, and Krikey incorporated this more dynamic, creative style into their visual marketing materials.

Finally, the company found out that many users referred to their app not as an "AR app" but as a "3D app." They swapped out the word AR for 3D, and again, saw a more positive reception.

Recognizing that they wouldn't have gained this critical human insight without user testing, Krikey has continued to run Google Play Store user tests every few weeks and make tweaks as suggested by users. Due to continual health checkups, their app install rate has increased 45% in six months.

# A recommended approach: Observe people as they engage with a particular part of the customer journey.

**Objective:** Improve and optimize critical parts of your experience, especially for flows that impact KPIs.

### Step 1: Ask a user to complete an activity related to a point of interest on the customer journey.

There is no shortage of key interactions that you should be pulsing regularly, and these interactions range from digital to physical and everything in between. When considering the core parts of the long-term customer experience, you can gather human insight on:

- **The path to or point of conversion.** Whether it's a shopping experience with a checkout flow, an app store browsing experience that results in a download, or a financial services product comparison that leads to an application, you should be looking at these key experiences regularly.

- **Initial experience.** How do people react to your experience the first time they see it or interact with it? Are they overwhelmed? Do they want to engage immediately? Or something in between? Keeping a regular pulse on that initial experience will help you further optimize and drive adoption. This can be everything from your welcome email to unboxing a physical product.

- **Ongoing use and adoption.** Think about the key ways your customers engage with you once they've come on board and had an initial experience with you. What keeps them coming back? And how do you optimize those experiences? For example, if you are a mobile provider, you likely want to keep tabs on how your customers pay their bills, add new features or devices, or upgrade their existing products and services.

- **Customer support.** Poor customer support experiences can really irk your customers. Regardless of what support mechanisms your company employs, test the process of accessing support. In a user test, ask users to try to engage with chat, locate the help line phone number, or grab a rep's attention via Twitter.

## Step 2: Observe them as they walk through the process and listen as they narrate their observations and interactions.

There's a lot that happens at a rapid pace during a user test. Consider these questions as you observe and listen:

- When they are given an activity to complete, do they quickly know what to do and where to start? Or do they hesitate a bit?
- Are they able to move easily through the experience?
- Where are the snags?
- Can they find and understand crucial information as they proceed?
- Can they fill out forms or fields without any trouble?
- How long does it take for them to complete each step? The full process?
- What challenges or mistakes do they encounter along the way?

## Step 3: Ask them about the experience.

After they try different activities using the live experience, you will likely have questions for them. Some to consider are:

- **What worked well.** This will help the team understand what is working well now and what to retain in the experience.
- **What was confusing.** This will help the team identify perceived challenges and hiccups, as well as clarify what to focus on improving in your next iteration.
- **How they felt while using it.** They may have been able to zip through various activities, but if the experience was lackluster or didn't meet their expectations, you need to know that.
- **How confident they are that they did what you asked them to do correctly.** If they are wildly confident that they did all the activities given to them, but you noticed they didn't successfully complete most, that's a disconnect that needs to be addressed.
- **What they might improve.** Although customers don't always know what they need or what improvements are necessary, it can be helpful to gather this perspective. You may get some gems just by asking.

## Step 4: Share and take action on key learnings.

You'll likely walk away with tons of notes and ideas after watching just a handful of people using your experience. It's important you take action on key learnings. Try not to succumb to analysis paralysis. Here are some typical next steps after a user test:

- **Identify high priority issues to address.** Typically, a handful of issues will arise that everyone experienced. For example, everyone was confused by the pricing or no one could find the membership details. Determine the ones that were showstoppers and/or tied to business KPIs and get the team together to address. Once you improve your approach, you can user test again.
- **Log issues that may not be addressed right away.** Not everything you observe and capture can be addressed before the next iteration or

improvement. Capture these so you can look back over time to ensure they eventually get addressed. There's a good chance that many will go away over time as you pivot or shift your approach.

- **Plan for your next round of feedback.** With the issues you've captured, you'll likely need to make some improvements and you should build user testing into your plan. No experience is ever perfect. Your next round of feedback may be another user test of the improved experience or it could be a round of card sorting to address critical navigation challenges. (See page 119 for details on cardsorting.)

- **Share findings and accompanying video clips—both good and bad—with others.** What you observed, heard, and captured in your user tests should be shared. You can bring in lunch and have everyone watch the sessions together or you could get creative with the recordings and create a "highlights" and "lowlights" compilation to communicate what worked well and where the team needs to focus next.

## Data-Driven Investigation

**Why Is This Important?**   Health checkups on existing processes are open-ended explorations that may or may not reveal issues at critical conversion points. But when it comes to data-driven investigation, you're honing in on something specific. You've found a specific metric you need to better understand or a pattern in your data that needs further explanation. Your job here is to figure out exactly what's happening and how it should be addressed.

For example, if one of your key features isn't being used, you'll see that in your data. What's keeping them from using or interacting with this feature? Is it hidden or hard to use? Or do they just not see its value? If you don't investigate, you'll only be able to make educated guesses, which can lead to changing the wrong element and further obscuring the true issue.

It's perfectly natural to enter into this type of user testing with a hypothesis. You may think customers are dropping out of the checkout flow because it has too many graphic elements or asks them to enter more information than they'd like. But make sure you keep an open mind; the real reasons may surprise you.

Finally, it's tempting to narrow in on a single part of an experience as a way to shed light on the root issue or cause. We strongly recommend against this. Without the full context of how this single point plays into the overall experience, you will risk missing the problem altogether.

**Case Study: Large Global Retailer**   One of the largest global retailers noticed that a high percentage of their 600,000 daily website visitors were abandoning product detail pages at a rate higher than they preferred. The team had many hypotheses about why this was happening; some thought prices were too high, others believed that shipping wasn't fast enough, and some thought that there weren't enough details on the page.

Instead of solving for one of the hypothesized issues, the team put the website in front of actual customers and asked them to shop and browse. In doing so, they learned the real reason why customers were dropping off the product detail pages: The product imagery was lackluster, so customers couldn't gather sufficient understating of what the product looked like. And without this understanding, customers were going to other retailers for those details—and ultimately to convert.

After many design iterations—fueled by human insight—to improve the product imagery, the team pushed the updates live. Once live, the team saw a revenue lift of 13% on the website. After this win, the team continues to use human insight to improve the flows and experiences tied to conversions and revenue.

# A recommended approach: Observe people as they use the experience tied to the key metric you're trying to influence or learn more about.

**Objective:** Improve critical KPIs

**Step 1: Ask a user to complete the activity that is tied to the metric you're interested in influencing or learning more about.**

Businesses have a lot of data. Here are some examples of metrics you could influence with human insight at every critical step of the experience longtail.

- **The path to or point of conversion.** Customers are dropping off on product details pages or the 3rd page of an application flow, or aren't scrolling the entirety of an article that is meant to drive leads. Use customer perspectives to make informed decisions on how to reverse the drop offs.

- **Initial experience.** This can encompass everything from people downloading but not using your app to users subscribing and then unsubscribing quickly afterwards. In physical settings it may also include single-purchase customers. Whenever your data tells you that something is going badly awry when customers first interact with your business, it's time to user test.

- **Ongoing use and adoption.** You notice a trend of single-visit customers or large time gaps between use. Lack of repeat business is something that can affect every business model from food-ordering apps to news websites to car rental services. In order to understand how to get people coming back, you need to gather some customer perspective.

- **Customer support.** If you have a support team in place, they're likely flagging and categorizing issues as they are reported. Everything from comments on pricing shifts to opinions about new features may be flooding in from your customers. You may also be scraping social media and emails coming into the company. When you see trends in this data, you'll know where to focus your efforts.

### Step 2: Observe them as they walk through the process, and listen as they narrate their observations and interactions.

There's a lot that happens at a rapid pace during a user test of a specific flow or interaction. Consider these questions as you observe and listen:

- What is the end-to-end experience like? Even though you are focused on a particular page or element, it's important to understand how the overall experience impacts their behavior.
- For the particular page or element you're focused on, what happens when people arrive? Do they have trouble interacting with it? Are they confused about some content or copy? Why do they become disengaged or drop?

### Step 3: Ask them about the experience.

After they walk through the experience, you will likely have questions for them. Some to consider are:

- **What worked well.** This will help the team understand what is working well now and what to retain in the experience.
- **What was confusing.** This will help the team identify perceived challenges and hiccups, as well as clarify what to focus on improving in your next iteration.
- **Challenges with specific points or interactions.** You likely have a specific area you're interested in getting feedback on. Make sure you spend some time doing so.
- **What they might improve.** Although customers don't always know what they need or what improvements are necessary, it can be helpful to gather this perspective. You may get some gems just by asking.

### Step 4: Share and take action on key learnings.

You'll likely walk away with tons of notes and ideas after just a handful of people using your experience. It's important you take action on key learnings, especially those that are directly tied to the metrics you're working to influence. Here are some typical next steps after a user test:

- **Identify and fix the top issues tied to the key metric and address them.** Document the key issues that were showstoppers and tied to KPIs. Then fix them.

- **Log issues that may not be addressed right away.** Not everything you observe and capture can be addressed before the next release or update, especially if it's not directly tied to the metric you've trying to improve. Capture these so you can look back over time to ensure they eventually get addressed.

- **Share findings and accompanying video clips to provide the team with rich context.** You've likely identified a snag or two that is impacting customer behavior. Share the user test recordings with your team. Without this context, they won't truly understand the challenge. Added bonus: Seeing it with their own eyes will help them formulate the right solution and (hopefully) act with urgency.

- **User test the improvement before it's launched.** Make sure you've fixed the problem correctly before launching it. You can do this by putting a prototyped version in front of users to use and gather their perspective. The worst case scenario is that your fix further exacerbates the problem. Avoid that with user testing before launching the updates.

## Competitive and Best-in-Class Assessment

**Why Is This Important?** Running user tests of competitive experiences on a regular cadence will help you see how the competition is performing, but it can also help you identify opportunities for differentiation and understand how the landscape is changing over time.

And you don't need to just have your customers use competitive experiences. You could also have your competitors' customers use yours.

Imagine the insight you could collect from loyal Peets' customers if you asked them to compare the Peets app to the Starbucks app, and then asked loyal Starbucks users to do the same. You'd learn a whole lot about the competitive landscape and you'd be able to quickly identify ways to differentiate.

In addition to competitive analysis, you can user test best-in-class or preferred experiences. Ask users to give feedback on popular sites and apps or other companies who may not be your direct competitors but are known to provide exceptional experiences. Find out what users love about them and find ways to emulate that in your own experience. This type of input is valuable because people generally resist re-learning patterns. If you can mirror people's all-time favorite point-of-purchase or conversion flows, you'll make their experience far easier.

Modern customers are also quite opinionated about their expectations. They've got favorites, pet peeves, and particular organizations they admire for creating easy, seamless experiences—which means you can user test to align yourself with those preferences.

**Case Study: Mobile Phone Service Provider**   When the head of a top mobile network in the United States saw the annual JD Power rankings for his industry, he was borderline furious to discover that his company hadn't secured the number-one slot. He set a goal to move it up in the rankings.

The company began running competitive assessments on a monthly basis. They studied what other mobile phone service providers were doing well, what they were doing badly, and how customers felt about them. With this information accumulating over time, the company began to form a picture of how they could differentiate their offerings and pull ahead of the pack.

One sticking point among customers was clarity of pricing. As most people are painfully aware, mobile plan pricing is notoriously opaque and not something that can typically be fully explored on a provider's website. Customers disliked and distrusted this and many expressed a desire for clearer explanations and simpler plans. One of this company's competitors launched a streamlined and easy-to-decipher pricing strategy, including web pages with all the pertinent details, and customers loved it. When this company followed suit, they began to get similarly positive feedback.

The end result? By the next award cycle and after several rounds of strategic changes to their offerings based on human insight—this mobile network was ranked number one by JD Power.

# A recommended approach: Observe people as they interact with a competitive or best-in-class experience.

**Objective:** Find ways to optimize your experience and differentiate from the competition.

### Step 1: Ask a user to complete an activity on a competitive or best-in-class experience.

Consider getting perspective on the critical parts of your competitors' or best-in-class customer journeys, including:

- **The path to or point of conversion.** Virtually every modern business has an element of their path to or point of conversion experience with a set of standards or best practices. Browsing, shopping, purchasing, registering, creating an account, making a payment, etc. The list is endless. Understanding what to emulate and what to avoid can make or break your conversion metrics.

- **Initial experience.** As with conversion points, user testing the initial experiences that customers have with other organizations can help you make informed choices about how to improve yours. To gather information on initial customer experiences with best-in-class businesses, ask users to give feedback on companies who may not be your direct competitors but are known to provide exceptional experiences. Find out what users love about their initial experiences with those businesses, and incorporate elements into your own onboarding or welcoming process.

- **Ongoing use and adoption.** If it's publicly available, you can user test it. Imagine you are a top retailer and you want to understand what your competition is doing to drive engagement and loyalty. You can user test that! And think about some notoriously sticky experiences like Instagram or Robinhood. What makes them so sticky? How can you emulate those tactics in your experience?

- **Customer support.** Watch what your competitors are doing to offer ongoing support to their customers. Where do they show up? Does their support meet customer expectations? How does it compare to your support experience? Also, consider gathering feedback on companies that excel at customer support, even if they are outside of your industry.

### Step 2: Observe customers as they use the experience and listen as they narrate their observations.

As they interact and react, consider these questions:

- How does your experience compare to the competitive or best-in-class experience?
- How do they react and respond when they come to points in the experience that differ from yours?
- What works well in the competitive or best-in-class experience? What doesn't?
- Where are the particularly painful moments? Where are the delightful ones?
- Where are the gaps? What's missing?

## Step 3: Ask customers directly about their experience.

After they've used the competitive or best-in-class experience and shared their feedback, you'll likely have more questions. Here are some areas to explore:

- **Your experience against a competitor's.** How does your experience compare to the competitive experience? You may have your opinions but ask for customers' perspectives.

- **Competitive strengths and weaknesses.** Where does the competitive experience excel? Where are the difficult parts? Knowing what you're up against and finding ways to differentiate is a valuable perspective to capture.

- **Delightful moments.** With best-in-class experiences in particular, there are moments of delight that you can learn from. Ask for opinions on what worked exceptionally well. As we've noted, your competitor can be the last great experience a customer has had.

## Step 4: Share and take action on key learnings.

Competitive and best-in-class assessments can result in a lot of data to parse. Try not to spend too much time in the weeds. Find your key learnings and come up with a plan. Some actions that may result in this type of user test include:

- **Address high impact (and preferably low effort) changes.** You may find that your competitors are offering a valuable solution that your customers are eyeing. Or you may find that your checkout experience does not emulate the best-in-class checkout experience. Identify and address issues that will impact key metrics.

- **Influence and inspire the teams that support the overall customer journey.** You've likely learned a lot about yourself, whether by comparing yourself to your competition or learning how you measure up to best practices. Do a readout of your findings—especially the ones that are bigger and broader and not so tactical—with the teams responsible for them. Find the right leaders and share this feedback to influence change.

- **Capture your takeaways.** Since we recommend doing this on a regular basis, you should be keeping tabs over time. Looking at your competitor's experience on a quarterly basis should result in some meaningful insight over months or years.

## Customer Journey Tracking

**Why Is This Important?**   When you run a user test, you're likely isolating a single aspect of the customer experience to gather feedback and make improvements. But the customer doesn't experience anything in isolation in the real world. The challenges that they encounter and the decisions that they make when interacting with your company happen on a continuum and, sometimes, over a long period of time. So if you don't take a step back and user test *the entire customer journey*, you won't be able to improve the holistic experience for them.

By observing customers and prospects—from initial perception to final steps in their decision making process—you're in the passenger's seat in understanding the customer journey. And these insights can help you generate ideas on what to change.

**Case Study: Leisure Travel Company**   When a US-based leisure travel company released a new product offering that allowed customers to curate their own travel packages, the company saw an influx of customer support calls and chats from people using it.

The main reason why people were contacting the company was because they didn't think they could customize their flight selection during the booking process. To understand what the specific challenge was, the team user tested it. They learned that customers would hover over a certain part of the page expecting an option to customize their flights, but the site didn't provide that option.

Based on the learnings, the team added a link to customize flights where customers expected it during the booking process. Once the changes were live, the team saw an increase in travel package bookings and an 82% reduction in support calls.

# A recommended approach: Capture what it's like to be a customer over multiple touchpoints.

**Objective:** Optimize the experience across channels and devices.

### Step 1: Ask a user to complete an activity that spans multiple touchpoints.

From awareness to research, conversion, and beyond, all the interactions your customer has with you add up over time. Thankfully, you can capture this holistic experience via user testing. Some tips to make this happen:

- **Follow the same people over time, channels, and key journeys.** When you are finding people to include in your user test, ask them if they'd be willing to share their feedback on more than one experience. The commitment could be hours, days, weeks, or beyond, so it's important to get that upfront commitment. Also consider including more people than you need as you tend to see dropoff over time, especially with commitments beyond a week or two.

- **Ask them to document the experience from their perspective.** In these sessions, you are usually not following along in real time. Instead, you start them on a path or activity and ask them to capture the experience over time. They can do this by taking pictures, recording themselves, keeping notes in a document, and/or answering specific questions.

- **For the most part, let them choose how and where they want to interact with the company.** The beauty of this approach is that the customer chooses their own adventure. You may give them a broad activity, such as finding a new mattress, ordering it, and using it over the course of a month. How the customer chooses to research, purchase, and get the mattress is entirely up to them, and you will see lots of unique paths this way.

- **Consume as it comes in.** These approaches tend to generate a lot of data. Try to consume as it comes in since it can be overwhelming if you wait until the end. Also, this gives you the opportunity to provide additional instructions if you need to course correct. You can't do this after the fact.

- **Include regular check-ins.** Whether it's through a regular conversion, daily or weekly prompts, or a touchbase at the start and end of the user test, make sure you communicate and connect with the people in your user test. You can get richer, more contextual feedback during these sessions, but most importantly, it helps with keeping folks engaged—especially if you're asking them to capture their experience over a longer period of time.

### Step 2: Observe them as they walk through the process and listen as they narrate their observations and interactions.

In this type of user test, you'll watch people shift between channels, devices, and environments. Consider these questions as you observe and listen:

- What is the end-to-end experience like? Where are the high points? Where are the low points?

- When do they typically engage? Is it certain times of day? Certain days of the week?

- Who else is involved throughout the process or at certain points?

- What resources or experiences do they use beyond yours?

### Step 3: Ask them for their feedback along the way and when they're done.

Through regular check-ins with the people in your user test and with a wrap-up conversation at the end, you can ask for more feedback. Some topics you'll likely cover include:

- **What worked well and what didn't for each interaction.** This will help the team understand what is working well now and what to retain in each touchpoint. It will also help the team identify perceived challenges and hiccups as well as what to focus on improving in the next iteration.

- **How and why they chose to engage in certain ways.** You may see the majority of the interactions took place after 9 p.m. on mobile devices. Understanding why will help you build more understanding about your customers and their needs.

- **The highs and lows of the end-to-end experience.** What stood out to customers as being a "great" part of the overall experience? What parts were most challenging? This insight will help you understand feelings and sentiment across the journey, and it will help you prioritize issues to address.

- **What they might improve.** Although customers don't always know what they need or what improvements are necessary, it can be helpful to gather this perspective. You may get some gems just by asking.

### Step 4: Share and take action on key learnings.

When you track a person over a period of time and across key interactions with your company, you're going to capture a lot of feedback and action items. It's important you take action on key learnings. Try not to succumb to analysis paralysis. Here are some tips for taking next steps and action:

- **Narrow in on or confirm problematic issues.** Because the people in the user test may take different paths, strong patterns may not emerge. If someone had a particularly poor experience, you may run another user test with a few more people to hone in on the issue. Or you may choose to address it regardless.

- **Document the journeys.** It's best to show the various paths people took to complete an activity. With each touchpoint, list out what worked well and what needs to be improved, and include the customer's overall sentiment. Attach video clips from the user test to bring these touchpoints to life, too.

- **Bring the journey to life through video and circulate it.** This user testing approach is perfect for storytelling as teams can watch a customer as they make their way through a journey. For example, setting up a shipment, dropping off the package, and tracking it until it arrives is a narrative that will captivate viewers. Make sure you package it up in a digestible way and distribute.

# PART 4

# The Culture Shift: Applying Human Insight at Scale

In this final section, we offer strategies around infusing the practice of user testing into your entire company. Human insight gleaned from user tests should become an integral part of your corporate culture. Otherwise, you can't cultivate that all-important shared understanding of the people you serve or truly center the customer in every discussion, activity, and decision. User testing and the human insight it yields should be a constant presence.

With that in mind, we've offered strategies for two approaches: creating a groundswell of support among multiple departments through a grassroots movement or by promoting and driving human insight from the C-suite. Naturally, we hope you won't just take one approach or the other, but marry them together so this culture shift can happen organically and quickly.

# CHAPTER 10

# Bottom Up

## The Grassroots Movement

Annie Corbett, senior manager of user research at digital sports entertainment and gaming company, DraftKings, knew her company would benefit from widespread user testing and the dissemination of customer perspectives. She was on a mission to arm all members of the organization with actionable human insight so she could equip them to make better, more informed business decisions.

But her colleagues within the company had questions, and a few did not fully understand the potential of obtaining this insight. How could DraftKings employees talk to customers quickly and easily? How would they be able to keep pace with the speed at which the product team builds? Would teams really act on these insights if they had access to them? Could feedback be shared in a way that didn't totally overwhelm everyone?

For a company that sees large, sometimes triple digit customer growth, it's important that the organization has a close ear to the ground, ensuring customer feedback is being considered and users are enjoying the products that DraftKings offers. DraftKings already had, and still has, a highly analytical culture, so Corbett's main challenge was to prove that user testing wasn't just valuable, but indispensable.

Annie knew she needed to breed curiosity through awareness and communication of her ideas, and by doing so, she created a groundswell of interest. With some quick wins under her belt, she began to involve more teams and business functions in user tests, recruiting internal advocates as she went. Now, DraftKings has integrated human insight into its product development cycle, built an extensive library of key learnings and illustrative video clips developed, a state-of-the-art research lab in their downtown Boston headquarters, and cultivated an iterative design culture fueled by customer feedback.

Corbett made all of these changes from the ground up. Yes, she was a leader within DraftKings, but not a member of the C-suite. She wasn't the one signing paychecks and approving budgets, and yet she still found ways to instill cultural change.

You can do the same. No matter who you are within your organization, if you're the person who sees clearly that everyone will benefit from access to user tests and the human insight they generate, you can start the discussion. You can get the gears turning that will lead to a cultural shift at your company.

But, like Corbett, you may face dissenters, disbelievers, and challenges along the way. So we've structured this chapter to prepare you for the most common ones, offering strategies to navigate all of them effectively.

Here's what you might come up against if you're trying to create a grassroots movement around user testing and human insight.

# If You're Working in an Engineering-Centric Culture ...

Plenty of companies end up with cultures that defer to engineers when it comes to conceptualizing and creating products. Instead of starting with input from customers or guidance from product managers, the engineers tend to take the lead and pursue the concepts that focus on meeting technical requirements.

And since engineers think like engineers—like people who build stuff from scratch and understand the intricacies of complex systems—the concepts they favor are often counterintuitive to laypeople. There's a mismatch between the mental models of the person doing the building and the person it's being built for that can lead to finished products working in ways that customers don't expect. Or like.[1]

If you're facing this challenge, you're in good company. Microsoft's culture was historically engineering-focused, but that changed with Satya Nadella at the helm. He specifically asked his employees to "invoke our ability to meet unarticulated or unmet needs." And since internal teams seek customer input throughout key steps, the company has successfully reduced the risk of product failures and made consistently faster decisions.[2]

"If you're not learning from your customers, then you're probably not going to make a product that meets their needs," explains Tom Lorusso, Xbox Principle User Research Manager at Microsoft. "We view user research as a way to build confidence throughout the product development cycle."

---

[1]Don Norman, *The Design of Everyday Things: Revised and Expanded Edition* (New York: Basic Books, 2013), 16.
[2]Satya Nadella, https://www.marketing-interactive.com/microsofts-satya-nadella-innovation-comes-from-having-a-deep-sense-of-empathy

So how do *you* shift your company's engineering-centric design culture to one that creates and refines offerings using customer feedback and input?

## Tip 1: Start Small

It's pretty common for an engineering-centric culture to endure in legacy companies. In these settings, including customer perspectives in the design-build process may feel very foreign and awkward, which means that transitioning to consistent use of user tests will need to happen over time. Don't try to boil the ocean here; instead, take small steps and be patient.

As we mentioned in Chapter 7, testing early in the development process is generally a best practice. But in this situation, we recommend integrating user testing toward the end of the development process, closer to launch. Doing this can be effective in changing attitudes toward user testing because it produces human insight that is actionable and direct. Engineers can tie customer input directly to important improvements that they can easily execute and, with each small success, they can begin to associate user testing with positive outcomes.

Don't adopt this tactic over the long term, though. It's a stopgap solution to ease your engineering-first culture toward valuing human insight and should be used only until you can pull user testing back into earlier phases of design and development.

## Tip 2: Give Newcomers to the User Testing Process the Support They Need

Once you've got a smidgen of buy-in, remove the barriers to user testing. Don't just get people to do it, help them do it efficiently and easily. Some ways to do this include: recruiting customers for the tests so teams don't need to hunt around for them, providing lists of questions to ask, creating reusable user test templates that teams can use at specific checkpoints, and offering checklists for running successful tests. But above all, find ways to integrate user testing into the tasks they're already doing. If you create a completely new workflow, you're just asking to be ignored. Be a good partner and set newcomers up for success.

## Tip 3: Find and Activate Internal Champions

Even in an organization that lets engineering lead product decisions, there will be individuals and groups who are eager to incorporate more user feedback. Find the people who are hungry for this change, and make them your champions. If you're in a company that works on lots of products simultaneously, seek out teams and leaders who *want* to be activated. Do a little sleuthing and handpick anyone who can help you talk up the benefits of user testing and the actionable human insight it generates.

Why bother doing this? Because it can't just be you, or you and your team, advocating for this cultural shift. You need to amplify other voices who are in favor of this approach. You need a group of people across the organization who can evangelize these ideas and become change agents. Ideally, this should include an executive sponsor who will work on convincing top leaders to get on board, but it should also include partners within engineering and development. You need someone on the inside of the group currently steering product development who already has the trust of their colleagues. This person can be pivotal in changing key minds and chipping away at calcified protocols.

We spoke to Jennifer Lee, who joined Wise (then TransferWise) in 2016 as their first ever qualitative researcher, and quickly saw she'd need the support of internal allies. She was hired for a standard UX researcher role—go and sit within teams, do their research and run user tests, help them integrate human insight into their work, and move the product forward.

But as is the case in so many companies today, she was hired alone, and there were no concrete plans at the time to expand the UX research team. The VP of Design who hired her knew Wise needed more research and design help, so created her role as an experiment to determine how user testing could be integrated into a very engineering- and analytics-heavy company.

The plan was to have her rotate among teams in Wise, staying with them long enough to provide insight and get them on their way, then jump to the next team that needed help.

But Jennifer's first project was a massive undertaking that had her working ten-hour days for six months, and she never felt fast enough or convincing enough to influence the project as much as was needed. She was burning out fast and the company was hiring even more product teams who would need her support. She knew while she was focused on one team, other teams were getting no help with human insight.

Jennifer saw that she needed to balance two goals at once: convincing the company at large that human insight was critical, and encouraging her colleagues to start performing user tests themselves.

She introduced Wise to the UserTesting platform, which delivered on the promise of simple and fast access to human insight. Getting insights back in under two hours was a game changer for her colleagues, and soon she had multiple teams eager to run their own user tests.

To manage the surge in demand, Jennifer held monthly training sessions where people could learn more. She invited everyone in the company and people from all teams showed up just out of curiosity— HR team members, analysts, engineers, product managers, and designers, to name a few. And many were amazed at how little they knew about the practice of user testing and how much their work would be improved if they utilized it.

This strategy worked beautifully and buy-in began to spread like wildfire. Teams that had worked with Jennifer before were telling other teams about their experiences, which led to more and more teams becoming interested in user testing and wanting to know how they can get the data they need.

Wise went from doing one set of customer interviews a month when Jennifer was a team of one, to running between fifteen and thirty user tests every week and at least five to ten customer interviews every month. Fifty of Jennifer's colleagues launch user tests on a regular basis, and Wise's UX research team now boasts twelve full-time researchers. As you can see, activating internal champions can lead to true change.

## Tip 4: Pull the Customer into Existing Processes

Reinforce successes and socialize changes by making user tests, human insight, and the course-corrections they enable part of everyday processes and where people already are. Spread the word by sharing stories across multiple media and platforms, in both large and small ways.

At Humu, a company helping teams to build habits that improve engagement and performance, product meetings begin with a quote, clip, or story that brings a customer to life. The success of this led them to introduce a regular "customer empathy" section in one of their company-wide meetings, giving leaders at all levels the chance to recognize the value of user testing, build empathy, and implement feedback from customers. This practice also creates fabulous opportunities for interdepartmental collaboration. As Marieke McCloskey, former UX Research Lead at Humu, shared: "The sales team knows a slice of the story, the product team has a different perspective, the customer success team has their view—and the process of bringing the customer story to life can tie it all together."

## Tip 5: Link Testing to a Business Result

Since the successes of engineers (and others who develop products) are often measured by metrics like adoption, sales, and ongoing engagement, those teams are more likely to embrace activities that support business impact. If you can illustrate how user testing ladders up to positive responses from customers, increased spending, long-term loyalty, word-of-mouth promotion, or anything else that impacts those metrics, you'll have a much easier time convincing engineers to get on board. Show them how human insight can help them and the company be more successful, and suddenly user tests will become a must-have and not a nice-to-do.

# If There's a Team That's Protective of User Testing …

If you work in a company that already runs user tests on a regular basis, there may be a nucleus of people who run those tests. They may be trained formally to do so and feel ownership of the process. As the entire company wakes up to the importance of human insight, there will be a demand for user testing that will require some of this work to be done outside of this nucleus of experts. These (often) protective teams aren't digging their heels in for no good reason; In all likelihood, they've spent years developing their craft and are worried that untrained colleagues may inadvertently introduce errors or bias.

Your challenge will be to both leverage their expertise and show them that other teams can also talk to customers and gather input without completely screwing it up. You need them to see the impact these learnings and perspectives can have on the business at large so they'll feel safe relinquishing just a bit of control.

## Tip 1: Make Protective Stakeholders Your Allies

First off, recognize and acknowledge that this nucleus of people possesses specific and highly valuable expertise. Don't go charging in and telling them they must let anyone and everyone run user tests. Or worse yet, task them with training others to do that work. Exercise diplomacy by pointing out that you can't run valid user tests without their support and input. Be firm about expanding the ranks of who can talk to customers directly, but involve these stakeholders in that expansion.

Then, help folks in the nucleus understand your process and needs. You may have certain ideas about how testing will fit into your work-flow that they can improve or tweak. Their knowledge and experience mean they'll have expertise about when and where to pull in human insight to share. Talk through your plans and ask for their help in refining your procedures.

## Tip 2: Include Protective Stakeholders in Your Wins

When announcements are made and customer stories are shared across the company, give those protective stakeholders a shout-out. Help them elevate their work and talk about its value. This is a group that can be under the radar, especially in younger companies, so getting them exposure and accolades will help keep you in their good graces.

Keep in mind, too, that people who conduct surveys, interviews, and other customer research are often measured on efficiency versus out-comes. This means that pulling your protective stakeholders into value conversations helps other people within the organization recognize their contributions. If you can say, "We launched this new product based on learnings we collected through user tests, using techniques recommended by this group," you're adding to their cachet.

## Tip 3: Offer Ongoing Support to Protective Stakeholders

For expert user testers, transitioning to a culture where nearly anyone can run a user test can feel downright scary. They know how easy it is to skew results and misrepresent data. They worry that some teams may run user tests just to confirm their own opinions. It's hard to watch a finely tuned craft get botched.

You can mitigate these concerns by turning your protective stakeholders into mentors. Pair an existing expert with someone who is just learning about the user testing process. Create an approval flow that threads your testing plans through their group for input. If you plan to assemble tutorials or guidebooks, partner with them on creating and editing the content. Their protectiveness comes from a good place. Leverage that urge and keep them involved.

# If Your C-Suite Is Reluctant ...

Executive leadership may hesitate to support a cultural shift toward consistent user testing and collection of human insight for any number of reasons. Historically, this work was slow and expensive, and although that's no longer the case, they may still worry about costs and efficiency.

On a related note, the C-suite is often acutely aware of the high price of big data collection and may question the need for collecting even more customer data on top of it.

And, depending on their background and perspectives, some business leaders may not believe that customers actually know what they want; they may feel safer deferring to internal experts than consulting the public when it comes to making critical decisions.

So how do you bring them around?

## Tip 1: Remove Executives from the Details

Executives are somewhat legendary for having packed schedules and short attention spans, so don't bog them down with all the use cases and processes. Focus on learnings and compelling human insight. Skip the fifty-page reports and offer them something simple and digestible like a one-pager, a video clip from a user test, and some recommended next steps. Show them how human insight have already had a positive impact on the company, and hit them with something emotional, memorable, and authentic.

## Tip 2: Help Executives Build an Emotional Connection to the Customer

While it can be helpful to shield reluctant executives from details, there is a flip side; they may benefit from observing the actual process in action. It's quite possible they feel reluctant to commit to consistent user testing because they have no personal or emotional connection to the technique. If you have them attend some sessions, view some particularly affecting videos, or find another way to expose them to user tests that are emotionally evocative, that can go a long way toward convincing them to buy in.

Watching and observing real customers changes people, particularly in scenarios that can be emotionally charged. Retirement, wedding planning, and sending kids to college may come immediately to mind, but there are many other situations that can be emotional, aside from the obvious ones. Depending on context, everyday activities and experiences can make feelings rise to the surface, and when executives get to witness that—to see how excited people get, hear their visceral reactions to a new feature, or observe how upset they feel when they can't complete a task—it impacts their understanding of how important user tests truly are.

The co-author of this book, Janelle, knows this from personal experience. She was working with a telecom provider who was testing a new concept: asking customers to install their own cable boxes. The company was hoping they could send out fewer technicians to customer homes, and if users could use the website to guide them through the setup process that would reduce costs. They brought in multiple groups of customers to test their overall reactions to the idea, and also to make sure the instructions provided were clear enough to make self-installation possible.

Janelle was sitting with the team and a handful of company leaders behind a one-way mirror in a lab setting, observing the user tests. Customers had various reactions to the self-install proposition, and gave some helpful feedback on the instructions, but nothing of note had happened until an older woman came in and changed everything. She pulled up the web page with the installation instructions and the moderator asked her if they seemed clear or confusing, at which point she began to cry. She apologized profusely, explaining that her husband had died a month prior and this was just the kind of thing he would've handled.

"I've never had to deal with this stuff by myself before," she explained through her tears.

Behind the mirror, you could hear a pin drop. Everyone was both surprised and affected by witnessing her reaction. Janelle could tell they were reevaluating their plan to ask customers to handle installation without support from company experts.

Janelle could tell that none of the people who'd seen this woman's honest and raw reaction would ever forget the experience. And she also suspected that—as experiences like this often do—it would impact how this group of company leaders viewed their customers in the future. Seeing user tests in person, especially ones that prompt genuine emotions, helps executives recognize customers *as people*. It becomes part of the knowledge and narrative that gets built up over time about your customers.

## Tip 3: Link the Effort to a Business Result

The performance of business leaders is gauged by metrics, so tie user testing to something they care about. Show them the value of this process and illustrate its power. We recommend doing this through storytelling and case studies, weaving stats and numeric results throughout a narrative. This allows you to show a stumbling block, a fix suggested by customers, and how the recommended improvement has driven sales or increased customer satisfaction.

## Tip 4: Understand Your Stakeholders

Tabitha Dunn, Chief Customer Officer at Ericsson, strongly recommends working to understand your stakeholders in the same way you understand your customers. Dunn has built customer experience practices from scratch at multiple companies, including Citrix, SAP, Xerox, and Philips, and knows that getting buy-in from executives only happens when the pitch is tailored to their decision-making styles and unique mindsets.

"You have to think about two things to be successful in a CX-related role," she says. "The first is why your customers do what they do. And the second, which too many people overlook, is why our own people do what they do. That includes internal teams, leaders ... everyone within the company."

Dunn has seen many of her colleagues get burned out in their roles because they show up with meticulously crafted artifacts such as journey maps that reveal where the experience is breaking down, but they can't seem to get the leadership support they need to pursue fixes. She believes this is because presentations to leaders only include customer perspectives and aren't created with the priorities, investment practices, and mindsets of the teams or leaders.

"Why would you treat your peers and senior leaders any differently than your customers?" she asks. "Turn those amazing customer insight skills internally to develop your key stakeholder insights, building a more successful case for change."

## If You Encounter General Resistance or Misunderstanding ...

A true grassroots movement is inclusive. That means everyone involved understands the value of a change and supports it wholeheartedly. So if you've got pockets of people in customer service or accounting who are apathetic about human insight, or the entire HR department believes user testing is expensive and wasteful, your work is not yet done. It's common for a few groups to resist, especially if they're unaware that user testing is valuable.

They may think it's complex, slow, boring, something that only trained experts can perform, or that it yields information that won't benefit them. They may worry that human insight will arrive too late in the process to influence it. It's not uncommon for people to have baggage attached to the idea of user testing.

That baggage must be addressed because your entire company needs to value and understand human insight. Stragglers need to become converts for this to be a true cultural shift within your company. So here's how you can change their minds.

## Tip 1: Make Hesitators Consumers of Human Insight

You definitely want teams from many business functions to run user tests if they so desire, but you also want to make it clear that some people can just consume the human insight being collected. Hesitators can watch the videos, listen to the stories at meetings, and absorb the findings on their own terms. Build more visibility around customer input, expose people to it, serve it up in a way that makes them want more.

Create stickiness around user tests so reluctant people will get excited about it. You can do this by sharing videos from user tests whenever you launch a new initiative. If you run a competitive study is run, tag interesting parts and circulate it. Stream live user tests in conference rooms and public gathering areas. Give them access to the results, the opinions, and the feedback your customers have provided so they can feel involved without actually running any user tests themselves.

## Tip 2: Call Out the Most Important Findings

If people are reluctant or resistant, you've got to make it easy for them. Focus on curating and bubbling interesting findings up to the top so they don't have to wade through endless videos or long reports. Point them toward the most relevant, unexpected, or critical tidbits of information.

## Tip 3: Make It Easy for Hesitators to Participate

As the cultural shift takes hold, people who once resisted user testing may become increasingly curious. You can transform them into active advocates by creating simple, approachable ways for them to interact with customers themselves or easily access additional human insight. Break down the barriers so they have opportunities to either do user tests or view user tests.

Microsoft did this by creating a "speed date" program where they set up a room with a handful of laptops, each of which had an open video feed to a real Microsoft customer. Team members could come in, sit down, and connect with the customer. The only effort the employees had to put in was showing up.

Whatever challenges you may face in convincing your colleagues to embrace user testing, don't let them overwhelm you. Changing corporate culture through grassroots organizing can be a slow process, but it's an incredibly effective way to initiate sustainable shifts.

When a philosophical or behavioral change has time to make its way organically from group to group, department to department or business unit to business unit, that means it's getting adopted at a pace that feels natural. No one feels like valuing customer input is some unexpected and sweeping mandate from on-high; they all get to mull the change, consider its benefits, and incorporate it into their working lives without feeling forced. That kind of groundswell is powerful.

And once it's begun, that's the perfect time for executives who value user testing to step up and begin championing cultural change from the top down.

# CHAPTER 11

# Top Down

## How Executives Can Support and Model Change

I f you're an executive, founder, or other business leader, you've undoubtedly heard the stories about Walmart founder Sam Walton dropping into his stores unannounced to walk the aisles and chat with workers.[1] Those stories are true and have morphed into the stuff of legend for a very good reason: that level of investment in empathy is rare.

Most top executives don't prioritize connecting with and understanding their customers and employees, and understandably so. Their time is extremely limited so everything must be ruthlessly prioritized. This is even more true now, as the business world becomes increasingly digitized and customers are further and further removed from the companies that serve them.

But a select few find ways to keep the customer top-of-mind, despite their heavy workloads. They carve out time to listen to user voices and absorb consumer feedback.

---

[1]https://money.cnn.com/magazines/fortune/fortune_archive/1991/09/23/75513/index.htm

Here's a great example: A while back, we met with the CEO of a home furnishing retailer in his San Francisco office. It was a gorgeous, airy space in the corner of a bustling office. As we sat on his couch and discussed the importance of connecting with customers, it became clear that he not only understood, but he had a real passion for it. He grabbed a letter off his desk to show us. The letter was three pages long and hand-written, sent to him directly by an elderly couple who'd purchased a couch. Apparently the delivery company had been late and rude and dinged a wall as they brought the couch inside. The couple was extremely upset.

We watched as he flipped through the pages, peering at the cursive scribbles in consternation.

"This just drives me crazy," he said. "This can't happen. We need to *fix* this."

While we never want to see business leaders feeling frustrated and stymied, it was pretty amazing to see one react with such genuine concern over a single buyer's experience. Clearly, he'd created the mechanisms necessary to receive letters like the one the elderly couple had written. He wanted those user concerns to reach his desk. He'd supported a culture that would put him in touch with the people who bought from his company because he wanted to know what they loved, hated, and wanted to change.

He embedded empathy into his role, actively and intentionally, so he could lead by example.

We know that many CEOs and VPs would love nothing more than to follow suit. They'd love to emulate Walton and "walk the aisles" of their businesses, cultivating understanding of their end-users and getting to know their workforce. They'd love to respond to customer concerns personally or ask employees about the issues they're facing. They just can't find the time.

Which is precisely why we're writing this chapter. There are dozens of ways for executives to both empathize with customers *and* help build a corporate culture around them that doesn't require shirking other duties or working nights and weekends.

And in order to consistently deliver the stellar customer experiences that win loyalty and increase market share, executives and leaders need to champion user testing and support customer-centricity beyond platitudes and promises, with meaningful actions. They need to truly sponsor a cultural movement that seeks, collects, and takes action on human insight.

The question, of course, is *how*?

How, as a leader, do you create a culture that organically and consistently supports user testing? How do you make sure everyone in the company understands and empathizes with the customer and works in response to that understanding and empathy? We've got some actions you can take to get the ball rolling.

# Tip 1: Build the Customer into Your Lexicon

Yes, we've already mentioned that saying you're "customer-centric" isn't enough, but saying you value customer input is an important place to *start* because language matters. Building customer needs, feedback, and understanding into the language used by people at all levels is something that will slowly but surely impact employee mindsets, and shifting the company lexicon is an initiative that business leaders can easily champion.

Consider building a phrase about your customers into the company mission statement and values, since these are the branded pieces of language that impact workers at every level. Use active language that centers on customer needs, ideas, feedback, desires, and lives.

And then, support those language changes with action. Don't just say it, give everyone at your company the opportunity to live it out!

# Tip 2: Maintain a Constant Campaign for Customer-Centricity

Once you've embedded customer-focused language into your company DNA and carved out some avenues for employees to listen to and learn from your customers, reinforce the importance of both. Repeat your values, laud the mission, and remind people to take advantage of the programs you've created. As a leader within the company, lead a constant campaign to keep customer-centricity top-of-mind.

Then underline those high-level messages by amplifying customer voices through storytelling. Open every all-hands meeting with a video of a user test or a written story about a customer's experience with your offerings. Include customer feedback in company-wide newsletters. Encourage the teams running user tests to share their findings as often and as broadly as possible.

And then? Reinforce the importance of user tests and the feedback they provide by holding your people accountable.

# Tip 3: Create Ways for People at All Levels to Connect Directly with Customers

According to UserTesting's 2020 CX Industry Report, only 33 percent of employees report that their organization has a proactive approach to CX.[2] While many leaders tout the importance of customer experience, teams aren't enabled to actually *be* customer-centric. You can make some intentional change here and fund programs that close the gap between lip service and action.

Catherine Richards, head of customer design at Tesco Bank, modeled this type of strategic creativity by helping her company launch a program that invited users into every level and department to share their feedback.

"About four years ago, we introduced Customer Wednesdays, a day dedicated to spending time with our customers face-to-face," Richards says. "Bringing customers into the building, having them sit in front of colleagues ... This was something that was quite new. But what we wanted to do was lower the barrier to our customers and really connect with them."

Customer Wednesdays led to some significant internal changes at Tesco Bank. For starters, the role of the design team shifted. This group was once seen as an add-on to other business functions, but once customer input began to infuse the company at large, design became central to the creation of new propositions, products, and

---

[2]https://info.usertesting.com/2021CXIndustryReport.html

physical spaces. The actual customer-facing sessions reached ninety per year in 2020, the equivalent of spending eighteen days face-to-face with Tesco Bank customers. Work done during Customer Wednesdays includes many approaches to user testing, and the company reports gaining around fifty new insights each year that directly support business cases.[3]

How your company approaches this will depend somewhat on size, industry, and budget, but there are multiple ways to offer your employees the chance to interact with and solicit feedback from the people they serve. Make it simple and easy for them.

# Tip 4: Link Customer-Focused Actions to Performance Standards

Here's where you move beyond lip-service as a leader. It may seem radical to tie customer-centricity and the implementation of user testing to hiring and performance evaluation, but we guarantee that doing so will transform the way your company does business.

Many organizations require employees to spend some time each quarter interfacing with customers, asking them to dedicate at least a few hours a month learning about the people they serve. These hours can be earned by observing or running user tests, but there are other means for connecting with customers, too. Employees can sit with members of the support department and observe them helping customers, or ask them about what they're hearing. Or they can speak directly to customers, ask them questions, interview them about their

---

[3]https://nilehq.com/customer-wednesdays/

experiences either in person or via video. A policy like this makes customer connection a must-do instead of a nice-to-do.

As a leader, you can also fold questions about the role of the customer into your orientation process. David Bolotsky, founder and CEO of online and catalog retailer Uncommon Goods, does this with everyone who joins the company.

"I meet with every single person that we hire," Bolotsky says. "Customer service team members, warehouse team members, everyone. And I ask them questions like, 'Who's the boss at UncommonGoods?' and they'll point to me and I'll say, 'No, follow the money. My name and my signature may be on your paycheck, but it's not my money we're talking about.' Eventually most of them will realize it's the customer's money, that the customer is the boss. I genuinely believe that we all work for the customer. We're reliant on word of mouth and repeat business. And so we've got to make sure we make our customers happy. And who controls that experience? We do."

Finally, since people do what is measured, incented, and celebrated, consider offering employee recognition for creating and supporting outstanding customer experiences. Rewards can be monetary, of course, or take the form of additional paid time off, gift cards, or other prizes. Highlight employees and teams receiving these accolades to broadcast how much you value their contributions and to encourage their peers to go above and beyond. Some companies create peer recognition systems to help further these programs. They build channels through which employees can send messages of thanks and nominate their colleagues for modeling the company's values, with nominations rolling up into scheduled drawings for prizes.

Now that you've linked customer-centricity to accountability, start building even more mechanisms that enable your people to keep users at the center of their work.

# Tip 5: Enable Teams with the Right Solutions

Business leaders must support and fund protocols and policies that help employees do right by customers. That means creating platforms for people to communicate, understand, collaborate, and consume information gathered from user tests. For example, shared resources, video clips from user testing runs, or a page on the intranet that lets them search for and view key findings.

But it also means moving beyond databases and embedding active processes that employees can leverage to serve their customers at the highest levels. Used car retailer CarMax did this by reconfiguring internal structures to emphasize both innovation and customer delight.

"We organized into small cross-functional product teams who are empowered with discovering solutions that customers love and will drive business results," says Jim Lyski, CarMax's CMO. "These teams operate like small start-ups within our large organization ... The objective is speed and low cost—which leads to low risk. We learn, perfect, and then continue the iteration process. The goal is fast learning and feedback—to get the consumer involved as fast as possible."[4]

Other organizations have created funding pools that support employees who see opportunities to create memorable customer experiences, and give those people the flexibility to take action when they see fit. The Ritz-Carlton hotels are renowned for their customer service and for employing people who go the extra mile for guests. In fact, every single employee, from housekeeping to management, can spend up to $2,000 a day per guest, to resolve issues or delight

---

[4]https://www.forbes.com/sites/kimberlywhitler/2016/09/25/the-next-generation-of-customer-centricity-a-methodology-to-drive-rapid-innovation/?sh=f1eacaf3f21c

customers, and are empowered to do so without asking permission from a supervisor.[5] This manifests in some truly extraordinary stories, like this one from Ritz-Carlton resort property Dove Mountain.

*... a family with a two-year-old son spent a weekend at the resort. As these guests were packing up to leave for the airport, the mom realized her son had lost his favorite Thomas the Tank Engine toy. Flagging down two frontline Ritz-Carlton employees, Jessy Long and Nathan Cliff, the guest explained what was at stake since this Thomas toy was her little boy's favorite and the loss would be heartbreaking for him.*

*Employees Long and Cliff failed to locate the lost Thomas train, but realizing how much this mattered to the guests, agreed together that something must be done. After the guests left the property for their flight home, the two employees drove to a toy store and purchased an absolute dead ringer of the original train for the little boy. They then composed a note in longhand to the boy in the voice of Thomas the Tank Engine telling a sweet tale about the extended vacation the little locomotive had taken after being accidentally left behind. The account included adorable pictures of Thomas exploring the property, cooking in The Ritz-Carlton kitchen (wearing a miniature paper chef's toque on his head), and more. Four days after the disappearance of the original Thomas, his replacement arrived by FedEx, to the astonishment of the family, who now share the story at every chance they find.[6]*

Another of our favorites is from Chewy.com, which was acquired by PetSmart in 2017. One of their customers had set up a monthly shipment of dog food and when his dog passed away, the customer received the next monthly shipment and clearly didn't have any use for it. After he contacted the company to set up a return, they refunded him and instead of asking him to send it back, they

---

[5]https://crm.org/articles/ritz-carlton-gold-standards
[6]https://www.forbes.com/sites/micahsolomon/2017/07/29/5-wow-customer-service-stories-from-5-star-hotels-examples-any-business-can-learn-from/?sh=1e5e00ba33e6

asked him to donate it. A few days later, he received a handwritten sympathy card in the mail alongside an oil painting of his beloved pup. Our guess is that, based on these actions, Chewy.com has a loyal customer for life.[7]

You don't need to give every employee a giant daily stipend or commission custom oil paintings for every customer, but you do need to build systems and solutions that help your people exceed customer expectations. Give them multiple resources and encourage them to be creative and empathetic in how they choose to create extraordinary customer experiences.

Then reinforce your desire for them to do so by centering customer needs in meetings and conversations.

## Tip 6: Ask About Customer Input and Feedback *Constantly*

As a leader in your company, you play a huge role in socializing ideas and behaviors. So model being inquisitive about the experience you provide.

We spoke with the CPO at a social networking service who is delightfully insistent on gathering user input on just about every offering. Any time teams pitch her a new idea or prepare to release a new feature, she grills them. "Did you user test this? What did people like? What did customers say about this?"

It seems so simple but just asking that question in meetings, making it part of the vernacular, and turning it into an expected element of every process has a massive impact.

---

[7]https://www.awesomeinventions.com/joseph-inabnet-chewy-refund-oil-painting/

Make it a common question that you ask your teams. Whenever you review a new rollout or offering, always ask, "What did users think?"

And then *listen*. Even if the news is bad and you have to scrap everything and go back to the drawing board, it demonstrates that you are putting the customer first. Take action on customer input or you're wasting your time gathering it in the first place. Show your internal stakeholders and customer base that you value honest feedback, and you'll be well on your way to cultivating an empathy-driven, customer-centric culture.

And finally, get your hands dirty and participate in the gathering of customer input.

# Tip 7: Put Yourself in the Customer's Shoes for *Real*

There's a huge difference between seeing videos of customers loving or loathing an experience and actually running a user test yourself. If you truly want to lead by example, be willing to get involved with user testing and gleaning human insight. Have conversations with customers *yourself* and share your findings with the company. This kind of modeling is absolutely priceless when it comes to proving your dedication to using input from the people you serve.

And, if possible, participate in the tests, too. Find out what it's like to be an actual customer for your company and put your offerings through the paces. Do it on a regular cadence, if you can, and encourage your peers in leadership roles to do the same.

A Fortune 50 retailer organizes a "Monthly Online Store Walk" with internal leaders as the testers and allows other employees to observe. The way it works is once per month, a senior manager, director, or other leader with an upcoming home project will share their screen and go through a shopping experience. In one of the first sessions, a senior director of product management wanted to update all the doorknobs on the second floor of his home. He used the mobile site to search for a close match to the knobs he bought for the first floor when his family initially moved in. Then he had to go through the process of selecting the types of knobs he needed (one-sided ones for closets, lockable ones for bathrooms, etc.).

According to an employee who attended this session, it was almost magical how many snags he hit, from missing purchase history details to inconsistencies in product collection details. More than fifty employees attended that session. And as word traveled, more attendees showed up. In the next session, the number of attendees had nearly quadrupled as compared to the first session.

"Monthly Online Store Walks" take place on Friday afternoons when employees are mostly done with work for the week, and they're extremely popular within the company. They're designed to be informal, sometimes funny, self-deprecating, and relatable. No one feels put on the spot or judged, everybody loves the chance to get face-time with leaders, and leaders enjoy being plugged in to the experiences they're responsible for sponsoring. These sessions are frequently referenced in later conversations among employees ("Remember how Dave couldn't do XYZ? It's like that ..."), proof that they build rapport while also giving leadership a peek into the user testing process.

Setting up a similar program within your organization will help you broadcast both humility and approachability. When people across the company can observe an executive walking through a user test, that underlines the importance of building great experiences using human insight. It also proves that leaders don't feel so far removed from their employees or customers that they can't participate in day-to-day activities.

One final note: Reinforce the message that the whole company is united in its efforts to gather and leverage customer input. Everyone's on the same team. It's easy for business units to feel competitive with each other, but one should never celebrate if another gets bad news from a round of experiments or interviews. Your whole company should be working toward creating and offering delightful, seamless experiences to your customers, and it's your job to make sure they do so as a single allied collective.

Great customer experience is a living, breathing relationship between a company and its customers, driven by an organization's continuous focus on the customer each and every day. Companies that succeed are the ones that develop deep customer empathy by constantly talking to their customers to explore and understand their worlds and their needs. Those efforts lead to customers who feel an authentic connection with their favorite brands and companies, and that connection drives loyalty and customer value.

In today's Experience Economy, putting your customer at the center of your business is no longer a competitive differentiator—it's a basic requirement. Having a usable, enjoyable, trustworthy experience that helps people achieve their goals is a necessity consumers have come to expect.

All businesses want to offer this type of outstanding experience to their customers, but not all of them succeed. What differentiates the leaders from the laggards is a dedicated focus to the customer experience across every possible touchpoint. World-class companies meet their customers where they are by listening to them, in their own words, and changing right along with them.

You can be one of those organizations. Your company can become a leader in customer experience just by committing to adding human insight to your approach. Whether you're a startup or a legacy corporation, you can close the empathy gap and support the people you serve by adapting to their authentic needs.

The best companies truly do put their customers at the center of their businesses.

Make sure *yours* is one of those companies.

# One Final Note

When we wrote this book, we were very careful not to make it all about our company. Yes, we run a technology platform that makes user testing easy and lightning-fast, but we wanted everything in these pages to be about the value of human insight, not the value of our single user testing platform. And we hope that intention shone through and that what you read was supportive, enlightening, and relatively objective.

That said, we know that you may need some additional guidance to implement your user testing practice, especially if you don't have mechanisms in place to support it today. So if you need more help, UserTesting is here for you.

We're extraordinarily good at what we do; we work with organizations of all sizes, and our video-first human insight platform is renowned for providing a vivid, first-hand view of what your customers are thinking and experiencing. Head over to usertesting. com to find out more, see additional case studies, explore our solutions, or launch a user test.

We'd be honored to be your partner in integrating human insight into your business.

# Index

2x2 matrix, usage, 87f

**A**
AAA Club Alliance (ACA), customers (connection), 23–24
Account teams, usage, 72
Affinity diagramming, usage, 85–88
Age of the Customer in the Experience Economy, 9
Airlines, customer hatred, 6
Analytics, usage, 11, 25–26
App download experiences, company obsessiveness, 151
Approval flow, creation, 184
Assets, customer preferences, 143

**B**
Best-in-class assessment, 162–164
Best-in-class experience
  activity completion, 164–165
  customer observations, 165
  learnings, sharing/action, 166–167
  observations, 164–167
  questions, 166
Bezos, Jeff, 100
Biased questions, avoidance, 55–56
Bias, omnipresence, 76–78
Big Data, usage, 29f, 31f, 33f
Bolotsky, David, 197
Brands, customer experience (revenue increase), 6–7
Business
  human insight, relationship, 97
  leaders, frustration, 192
  priorities, balancing, 110
  results
    culture shift effort, connection, 187
    testing, connection, 182
Business-to-business (B2B) companies, user testing, 71–72

Business-to-business (B2B) models, 151–152
Buyers, understanding, 121

**C**
Cardello, Jen, 100–101
  Product Development Framework, 101f
Card sorting, usage, 118–120
CarMax, internal structure reconfiguration, 198
Carvana, idea/impact, 12–14
Checkout
  experience, digital team responsibility, 22
  processes, company obsessiveness, 151
Chewy.com
  acquisition, 199–200
  customer loyalty, 200
Choosers, users (contrast), 68
Citrix, customer experience practices, 187
Cliff, Nathan, 199
Closed card sort, usage, 120
Communication, conversion points (optimization), 144–145
Companies
  culture, talent attraction/retention, 18–20
  customer-centric perspective, customer disagreement, 150
  customers
    contrast, 63, 65
    interaction process/location selection, 168–169
    perceptions, 143
  operating costs, increase (justification difficulty), 38
  questions, relationship/understanding, 44–46

Comparative Usability Evaluation
(CUE) investigations, 76–78
Competitive analysis, 163
Competitive assessments,
153, 162–164
Competitive experiences
activity completion, 164–165
customer observation, 165
learnings, sharing/action, 166–167
observations, 164–167
questions, 166
Competitive experiences, user
tests, 162–163
Competitive positioning, compari-
son, 142–144
Competitive strengths/weak-
nesses, 166
Consumer feedback, absorp-
tion, 191–192
Content issue, 91
Contextual signals, 82–84
Contributor Network (online
panel), 70
Conversion points, 155, 160, 164
optimization, 144–145
Corbett, Annie, 175–176
Cornell, Brian, 15
Costs, lowering, 18
Craigslist, usage, 71
Creative content, compari-
son, 142–144
Croften, Meg, 103
C-suite, culture shift reluc-
tance, 184–190
Cultural change, instilling, 176
Culture shift, 173
C-suite reluctance, 184–190
effort, business result
(connection), 187
hesitator participation, 189–190
Customer Experience, Three Es
(Forrester), 27–33
Customer journeys
documentation, 170
issues, logging, 157–158

observations/interactions,
narration, 156
people engagement, observation, 155–158
point of interest, 155–156
team support, influence/inspi-
ration, 166
tracking, 153
importance, 167–168
Customer resource manager
(CRM), customer data usage/
interaction, 25
Customers
acquisition, cost, 7
company
contrast, 63, 65
detachment, 17
sub-par understanding, 3
concepts/ideas, review, 113–116
customer-centric actions, human
insight (impact), 41
customer-centricity, campaign constancy (maintenance), 194–195
customer-focused actions, connection, 196–197
data
company collection/sorting/inter-
pretation, 7
sources, limitations, 24–27
demands, shift, 10
differentiation efforts, 143
direct connection,
methods, 195–196
empathy, 181
engagement, 181
executives
connection, prioritization
(absence), 191
emotional connection,
building, 185–187
experience, 4
excellence, 203
questions, 157–158, 161
team ownership, 149
usage, observation, 160–162

feedback
  capture/analysis, 76
  categories, 69–70
  questions, constancy, 200–201
holistic journey. *See* Holistic customer journey
identification methods, 65
impact, 193–194
input
  questions, constancy, 200–201
  valuation, 193–194
interview, 104–106
  frequency, increase, 181
journey, continuation, 147
lists
  management, 72–73
  usage, 72
loyalty, 18
  cementing, 149–150
multidimensional nature, 39
narratives, metrics (pairing), 95
opinions, direct questions, 109,
  114–115, 143
options, display (order),
  113–114, 142
ordering/pick-up experience,
  comparison, 5
pantry organization, understanding, 102
patrons, contrast, 66–67
perspective, access process, 63
preferences, internal
  sharing, 115, 142
problem navigation, observation, 106–108
problem statements, validation, 108–110
product manager interactions, per-
  centages, 11
professional/personal networks,
  contrast, 66
profile, revisit, 94
reactions, narration (observation), 109
self-reported customer feedback, 78

suggestions, face value (understanding), 14–16
support, 156, 160, 165
  contact, 72
  interaction, 152
touchpoint capture, 168–171
type, multiplicity, 68
understanding, 201–204
voices (amplification), storytelling
  (usage), 194
Customer Wednesdays, introduction, 195–196

**D**
Data
  capture/analysis, 75
  consumption, 169
  data-driven investigations,
    153, 158–162
    importance, 158–159
  patterns, extrapolation, 25
Databases, usage, 10
Decisioning
  human insight, integration, 18–19
  metrics, usage/problem, 16–17
Demographics
  examination, 67–68
  range, 68–69
De-Risking, 111, 112
Design thinking, 49–50
  framework, 50f
Digital experience, navigation/con-
  tent organization, 120
Digital team, actions, 22–23
Diplomacy, exercise, 183
Disney MagicBand, case study, 103
Disruptive issues, 93–94
Domino's Pizza, market share
  increase, 18
DraftKings, user testing, 175–176
Dunn, Tabitha, 187–188

**E**
Ease (customer experience compo-
  nent), 28, 30, 31f
Eavesdropping, usage, 79

Ecommerce infrastructure/supply chain, changes, 4
Effectiveness (customer experience component), 28, 29f
Efficiency, increase, 18
Email
  registration, 146
  signup process, 145–146
Emotion (customer experience component), 30, 32, 33f
Empathy
  customer empathy, 181
  embedding, 192
  map, 128f
Employees
  customer interface requirements, 196–197
  executives connection/understanding, prioritization (absence), 191
  manager context/information, 22
  satisfaction, erosion, 17
End-to-end experience, highs/lows, 170
Engineering-centric culture, 177–182
  design-build process, 178
  internal champions, finding/activation, 179–181
  process, customer engagement, 181
  user testing process, newcomer support, 178–179
Estes, Janelle, 186–187
Evans, Doug, 51
Executives
  details, control (reduction), 185
  emotional connection, building, 185–187
  empathy, 193
Experience economy
  competition, 3
  customer interaction, 10
Experience Economy, 203
Experiences
  company assessment, human insight (inclusion), 27–33
  creation, 19

customer questions, 146–147
derivation, customer understanding (impact), 11–14
feeling, description, 59
human insight, impact, 21
occurrence, 27
regular health checkups, 153–158
sketching, 108
team ownership, 149
user interaction, 145–146

**F**
FAQ redesign, 46
Feedback
  collection/gathering, 22, 53, 79–80, 92–93, 113, 142
  customer feedback categories, 69–70
  customer supply, 163
  impact, 58–59
  invitation, 66–67
  marketing team feedback, 51
  planning, 118, 148
  receiving, 90
  repositioning/tweaking, requirement, 93
  self-reported customer feedback, 78
  team validation/pushback, sharing, 110
  usage, 83–84, 112
  user feedback, 69
Forms, usage, 146

**G**
Gilmore, James H., 9, 27
Global retailer, case study, 159
Grassroots movement, 175, 188
Grassroots organizing, usage, 190
Guerilla intercepts, usage, 71

**H**
HelloFresh, cross-functional insight sharing, 36–38
High impact changes, 166
High-level messages, usage, 194–195
Hoggan, Ben, 112

Holistic customer journey
  human insight, usage,
    150f, 153–155
  initial experience, 151–152
  optimization, 149
  use/adoption, continuation, 152
Human connections, data valuation
  (comparison), 9–11
Human customers, fallibility, 78–80
Human insight
  action, 36–38, 89
  application, 173
  collection, 34, 36, 111
  consumption, hesitator change, 189
  customer information, 26–27
  derivation, 36
  examples, 29f, 31f, 33f
  human signal provision, 35f
  impact, 21, 41, 100–101
  importance, 16–17, 39–40
  inclusion, reason, 27–33
  overlooking/dismissal, rea-
    sons, 38–39
  playbook, relationship, 97
  presentation, creativity, 95
  types, user testing (impact), 90–94
  usage, 120, 150
  user testing, impact, 34, 36
Human signals
  contextual signals, 82–84
  interpretation process, 80–82
  progression, 82–83
  providing, 35f, 80–84
Humu, customer empathy, 181
Hybrid card sort, usage, 120
Hypothesis, proving (avoidance), 54–56

**I**
Ibarra, Herminia, 66
IDEA Center, 111–112
Ideas
  grouping, 86
  weeding, 113
Industry disruptors, 99
Inertia, innovation (impact), 3

In-product intercepts, usage, 72
Insider Insight process (Motivate
  Design), 79
"Insights Show, The," 36–37
Internal champions, finding/
  activation, 179–181
Interviews, conducting (prac-
  tices), 54–55

**J**
Juicero, failure, 51

**K**
Keeton, Ryan, 12
Key performance indicators (KPIs)
  impact, 155–158
  improvement, 145–147, 160–162
  usage, 116–119
Kodak, obsolescence, 17
Krikey
  case study, 154–155
  user opinions, 154

**L**
Leading questions, asking (avoidance), 54–56
Learnings
  application, location/process, 89
  incorporation, 106
  planning/application, consider-
    ation, 46–53
  sharing/action, 109–110, 115,
    118–119, 143–144, 147,
    162, 166–167
  socialization, 107–108
  tracking, 95–96
Lee, Jennifer, 179–180
  training sessions, 180–181
Leisure travel company case
  study, 167–168
Lexicon, customers (impact), 193–194
LinkedIn, usage, 70
Live intercepts, digital usage, 71
Local/domain knowledge personnel,
  consultation, 77
Long, Jessy, 199

Lorusso, Tom, 177
Low effort changes, 166
Lugar, Scott, 24
Lyski, Jim, 198

## M

Marketing, 121
  team, feedback, 51
Markets, creation, 99
Market share, increase, 18
Maxwell House, Robusta (introduction process), 63–64, 69
McCloskey, Marieke, 181
Mental models, mismatch, 177
Metrics
  activity, customer activity, 160–161
  customer narratives, pairing, 95
Mobile phone service provider, case study, 163–164
Molich, Rolf, 76
Monthly Online Store Walk, 201–202
Motivate Design, Insider Insight process, 79

## N

Nadella, Satya, 177
Net Promoter Score (NPS)
  company measurement, 53
  usage, 32
Network, usage, 71
Noise, sifting, 75
Notre Dame IDEA Center, case study, 111–112

## O

Offerings
  customer perceptions, 143
  decisions, problems, 17
  people, struggle, 91–92
  perspective, 92–93
  presentation, repositioning/tweaking (requirement), 93
  value, understanding (absence), 93–94
Ongoing socialization/ sharing, usage, 95

Online learning platform, expertise/ information compliation, 4
Open card sort, usage, 119
Organizations
  customer interactions, rating, 7
  humility/approachability, 202–203
Outcome-Driven Innovation (ODI) model, 103
Over-reporting/under-reporting, 79

## P

Panel companies, usage, 70
Pantry audits, usage, 39
Patel, Mona, 79
Patrons, customers (contrast), 66–67
Pediatric health system, case system, 115–116
Peet's Coffee
  insight, collection, 162–163
  Starbucks, comparison, 163
Peloton, ad backlash, 17
Perfect-fit users, connection process, 70–72
Performance standards, customer-focused actions (connection), 196–197
Persona, learnings (incorporation), 106
PetSmart, 199–200
Philips
  customer experience practices, 187
  mission, 194
Pine II, B. Joseph, 9, 27
Playbook, 97
Positive/negative framing, 54
Problems
  solving, importance, 102–104
  statements, validation, 108–110
Product Development Framework (Cardello), 101f
Products
  concept
    usage, propensity (determination), 114–115

value, determination, 114
creation, 99
  questions, 48–52
design iterations, 159
designs/prototypes, user testing, 116–119
development, 99
  human insight, impact, 100–101
  questions, 49–52
failures
  majority, 110
  risk, reduction, 177
improvement
  questions, 170
  user testing, 162
issues, logging, 157–158, 162
iterations, 115
launch, human insight (impact), 120
offering, creation (problems), 110
post-launch, questions, 52–53
questions, 161
teams, feedback (sharing), 144
trends/themes, decisions, 115
Professional/personal networks, customers (contrast), 66
Project Impact (Walmart), problems, 43–46
Protective stakeholders, involvement, 183–184
Prototypes, building, 51

**Q**
Questions
  asking, sharing intention, 59–60
  biased questions, advice, 55–56
  considerations, 46–52
  distractions, impact, 57–58
  excess, problem, 57f, 58–59
  focus, 56
  formulation/reuse, 61
  importance, 57–59
  leading questions, asking (avoidance), 54–56
  mapping, 45f

positive/negative framing, 56
  understanding, 44–46
  why questions, 60
  yes/no response, avoidance, 55–56

**R**
Regular health checkups, 169. *See also* Experiences
Richards, Catherine, 195–196
Rightness, question, 101
Right problems, solving (importance), 102–104
Right solutions, building, 110–112
Ritz-Carlton hotels, customer service, 198–200

**S**
Salesforce, customer information/relationships, 25
Salespeople, trustworthiness, 11–12
SAP, customer experience practices, 187
Self-reported customer feedback, 78
Session, capture, 36
Shared understanding (building), user testing (usage), 95
Shipt, usage/Target acquisition, 15
Shop-a-longs, replacement, 10
Shopping carts, company obsessiveness, 151
Signal, discovery, 75
Signup forms, company obsessiveness, 151
Snapchat (changes), user complaints, 17
Social-desirability bias, 78–79
Social platforms, 70
Solutions, building, 110–112
  approach, importance, 112–113
Southwest Airlines, customer valuation, 18–19
Spotify
  personalization, importance, 4–5
  success, 5
Spotify Warped, content (sharing), 5

Stakeholders
  allies, 183
  inclusion, 183
  support, offer, 184
  understanding, 187–188
Starbucks, Peet's (comparison), 163
Stickness, creation, 189
Sticky notes, generation, 86
Storytelling, usage, 95, 194
Surveys, information, 26

**T**
Takeaways, capture, 167
Target
  leadership decisions, 16
  omnichannel experience,
    creation, 15
  shopping experience, 14–15
Target audience
  people, discovery, 68–69
  user test, 67–68
Teams
  enabling, solutions
    (impact), 198–200
  user testing protectiveness, 182–184
  validation/pushback,
    sharing, 109–110
Tech-powered panels, usage, 70
Tesco Bank, 195–196
Text signups, usage, 146
Three Es of Customer Experience
  (Forrester), 27–33
Topline business driver, question
  mapping, 45f
Touchpoints
  activity, completion, 168–169
  customer capture, 168–171
  feedback, 169–170
  learnings, sharing/action, 170–171
  observations/interactions, nar-
    ration, 169
TransferWise, 179
Travel
  activities, impact, 149–150

efficiency/choice (improvement),
    customer fees (acceptance), 6
Trends, customer understanding, 8f
T. Rowe Price, case study, 145

**U**
Uncommon Goods, 197
Used vehicles, sales, 11–12
User experience (UX)
  problems, 91–92
  questions, 117–118
Users
  activity, completion, 116
  connection process, 70–72
  observations/interactions nar-
    ration, 117
  testing process, newcomer
    support, 178–179
  thoughts, narration, 116–117
User testing, 188
  ease, 205
  human insights, types, 90–94
  incorporation, 100
  issues (prioritization), 2x2 matrix
    (usage), 87f
  perfection, requirement
    (absence), 78
  team protectiveness, 182–184
  usage, 34, 36, 57, 53, 95, 116–119
User tests
  approach, mapping, 43
  human signals, examination, 82–84
  interpretation process, 80–81
  issues, grouping/prioritization, 77
  meaning (finding), affinity dia-
    gramming (usage), 85–87
  moderator, removal, 77
  people, selection, 67–70
  question, excess (problem), 57f
  recordings/notes/videos, review
    process, 80
  running, 81–82, 97
  sessions, analysis, 77
  videos, storytelling (usage), 95

## V

Value prop statement, usage, 143
Video clips, usage/sharing, 147,
158, 162, 170
Villacci, James, 36
Vocal complaints, 85

## W

Walmart store layout
customer survey, 43
Project Impact, problems, 43–44
question, 55
Walton, Sam, 191, 192
Why questions, 60

Wise, UserTesting platform,
179–180
Workflows, user testing (incorpo-
ration), 100
Worldview/inclusivity, expansion, 19
Wrap-up conversation, usage, 169

## X

Xerox, customer experience
practices, 187

Z

Zappos, customer loyalty, 18
Zendesk, customer information/rela-
tionships, 25